Using Corpora in the Language Classroom

CAMBRIDGE LANGUAGE EDUCATION
Series Editor: Jack C. Richards

In this series:

Agendas for Second Language Literacy *by Sandra Lee McKay*

Reflective Teaching in Second Language Classrooms *by Jack C. Richards and Charles Lockhart*

Educating Second Language Children: The Whole Child, the Whole Curriculum, the Whole Community *edited by Fred Genesee*

Understanding Communication in Second Language Classrooms *by Karen E. Johnson*

The Self-Directed Teacher: Managing the Learning Process *by David Nunan and Clarice Lamb*

Functional English Grammar: An Introduction for Second Language Teachers *by Graham Lock*

Teachers as Course Developers *edited by Kathleen Graves*

Classroom-Based Evaluation in Second Language Education *by Fred Genesee and John A. Upshur*

From Reader to Reading Teacher: Issues and Strategies for Second Language Classrooms *by Jo Ann Aebersold and Mary Lee Field*

Extensive Reading in the Second Language Classroom *by Richard R. Day and Julian Bamford*

Language Teaching Awareness: A Guide to Exploring Beliefs and Practices *by Jerry G. Gebhard and Robert Oprandy*

Vocabulary in Language Teaching *by Norbert Schmitt*

Curriculum Development in Language Teaching *by Jack C. Richards*

Teachers' Narrative Inquiry as Professional Development *by Karen E. Johnson and Paula R. Golombek*

A Practicum in TESOL *by Graham Crookes*

Second Language Listening: Theory and Practice *by John Flowerdew and Lindsay Miller*

Professional Development for Language Teachers: Strategies for Teacher Learning *by Jack C. Richards and Thomas S. C. Farrell*

Second Language Writing *by Ken Hyland*

Cooperative Learning and Second Language Teaching *edited by Steven G. McCafferty, George M. Jacobs, and Ana Christina DaSilva Iddings*

Using Corpora in the Language Classroom *by Randi Reppen*

English Language Teaching Materials: Theory and Practice *edited by Nigel Harwood*

Using Corpora in the Language Classroom

Randi Reppen
Northern Arizona University

CAMBRIDGE
UNIVERSITY PRESS

CAMBRIDGE
UNIVERSITY PRESS

32 Avenue of the Americas, New York NY 10013-2473, USA

Cambridge University Press is part of the University of Cambridge.

It furthers the University's mission by disseminating knowledge in the pursuit of education, learning and research at the highest international levels of excellence.

www.cambridge.org
Information on this title: www.cambridge.org/9780521146081

© Cambridge University Press 2010

First published 2010

A catalogue record for this publication is available from the British Library

Library of Congress Cataloguing in Publication data

Reppen, Randi.
Using corpora in the language classroom / Randi Reppen.
   p.   cm. – (Cambridge language education)
Includes bibliographical references and index.
ISBN 978-0-521-76987-7 – ISBN 978-0-521-14608-1 (pbk.)
1. Corpora (Linguistics)   2. Computational linguistics.   I. Title.
II. Series.
P128.C68R47   2010
407.1–dc22   2009052595

ISBN 978-0-521-76987-7 Hardback
ISBN 978-0-521-14608-1 Paperback

To my parents, Frank and Doris Reppen, who taught me to love languages and encouraged me to play with language.
Jeg elsker deg.

Contents

Series editor's preface

A major challenge in developing language teaching materials and resources has always been to provide learners with language input that accurately reflects the way language is used in the real world. Critics of traditional language teaching materials have rightly pointed out that the information they contain about the use of English – whether it be information about grammatical usage, vocabulary, or conversational discourse – has often been based on conventional wisdom or on the intuitions of materials' developers, information that was often inaccurate or misleading. The "authentic materials" movement in language teaching that emerged in the 1980s attempted to address this problem by advocating a greater use of real-world or "authentic" materials – materials not specially designed for classroom use – since it was argued that such materials would expose learners to examples of natural language use taken from real-world contexts. More recently the emergence of corpus linguistics and the establishment of large-scale databases or corpora of different genres of authentic language have offered a further approach to providing learners with teaching materials that reflect authentic language use. The present book provides a comprehensive yet very accessible introduction to the use of corpora in language teaching and will be welcomed by teachers and materials developers wanting to know how they can make use of corpora in their language classes.

Drawing on her extensive experience in developing and using corpora in language teaching, Dr. Randi Reppen offers a masterly survey of the nature of language corpora and their practical uses in language teaching. She provides numerous examples of how corpus-informed teaching materials can be developed and used in teaching at many different levels and with students in many different contexts. *Using Corpora in the Language Classroom* together with its companion Web site will enable teachers new to corpus-informed teaching to overcome possible inhibitions about the use of language corpora, and provides them with the essential knowledge, tools, and skills needed to make use of the rich resources made possible in language teaching through the use of language corpora.

Jack C. Richards

Preface

For many years I have been fascinated by corpus linguistics and how it can help me understand language better. My interest in corpus linguistics as a vehicle to better understand language has blossomed, and with that, a keen interest in how to use corpus linguistics to make me a more effective language teacher and teacher trainer. Corpus linguistics allows teachers and learners to be confident that they are learning the language they will encounter when they step outside the language classroom and into the real world of language use. Corpus linguistics provides a vehicle for bringing natural language into the classroom in a way that involves learners through hands-on activities interacting with "real" language. This book, *Using Corpora in the Language Classroom*, is designed to help teachers and teacher trainers better understand corpus linguistics and to help them bring the resources of corpora and hands-on learning with authentic materials into the language classroom.

Many teachers are eager to use corpora in their classrooms but lack the training and resources to accomplish this task. Teachers who would like to include corpus activities in the classroom are often overwhelmed by the task of locating corpora that are appropriate for their students, and by the task of creating activities for their students. This book addresses both of these challenges in four ways:

1. By providing an overview of corpus linguistics and detailed examples of corpus-based activities and materials, with case studies of class use that include hands-on activities.
2. By providing background information and principled instructions for creating a range of materials and activities that can be brought into the classroom, including how to create corpora to address specific class needs.
3. By providing lists of available corpora and Web sites that have corpus-based activities relevant to different teaching contexts and specific instructions on the use of existing Internet corpus resources.
4. By providing a companion Web site that includes links to online resources, frequency lists, and concordance lines (read Chapter 1 to find out what concordance lines are) as a springboard for activities; detailed corpus-based lessons and activities; and last but not

least, detailed instructions for using some of the more popular online corpora.

My goal in writing this book is to provide the step-by-step information needed for teachers to be able to successfully bring corpora and corpus resources into their language classrooms. All of the activities and examples in this book have been used in language classes. Every chapter has a strong hands-on component. Each chapter includes Your Turn boxes where you, the reader, are asked to interact with the material being presented or to do an activity.

Although only my name appears on the cover, this book certainly would not exist without the support and efforts of many people. A big thank-you to Don Miller for reading and commenting on portions of the book; your comments were very helpful. I owe a special debt of gratitude to Stacey Wizner who undertook the tedious task of combining my reference lists and standardizing the format of the Bibliography. I am especially grateful to Kathleen Corley who continued to believe in me and this project, regardless of the time zone that I was using for deadlines. A huge thanks to Carol-June Cassidy for her eagle-eye editing, helpful suggestions, and her positive energy. Doug Biber also provided tremendous support through engaging conversations on corpus linguistics. His confidence in me carried me through the ebb and flow of writing. Finally, thank you to the students in my MA, PhD, and ESL classes who have provided valuable insights that helped shape this book.

With such a multifaceted topic as corpus linguistics and using corpora to teach, there will always be aspects that are left unaddressed, but hopefully this book will serve to whet your appetite and curiosity for using corpora in your language classroom and provide you with some ways to accomplish this goal.

Randi Reppen

Acknowledgments

MonoConc Pro screen shots for Figure 1.1 on page 6 and Figure 1.2 on page 9 are used by permission. Thank you to Michael Barlow for allowing this use.

Figure 1.4 on page 15 from M. McCarthy and O'Dell, F., *Basic Vocabulary in Use* (Cambridge: Cambridge University Press, 2010, 7). Used by permission.

Figure 1.5 on page 16 from M. McCarthy, McCarten, J., and Sandiford, H., *Touchstone* Level 2, (New York: Cambridge University Press, 2004, 15). Used by permission.

Figure 3.1 on page 39, screen shot from R. C. Simpson et al., The Michigan Corpus of Academic Spoken English (Ann Arbor, MI: The Regents of the University of Michigan, 2002). Used by permission.

Figure 3.2 on page 40 and Figure 3.4 on page 46, screen shots from Mark Davis, 2008–, COCA: Corpus of Contemporary American English (400 million words, 1990–2009). Available online at http://americancorpus.org. Used by permission. Thanks to Mark Davies for allowing this use and for the great corpus resources that he makes available online.

Figure 3.3 on page 41 and Figure 3.5 on page 50, screen shots from Mark Davis, 2007–, *Time* Magazine Corpus (100 million words, 1920s–2000s). Available online at http://corpus.byu.edu/time. Used by permission.

Microsoft product screen shots reprinted with permission from Microsoft Corporation.

Table 5.1 on page 65 is excerpted from D. Biber et al., *Longman Grammar of Spoken and Written English* (Harlow, Essex: Pearson Education, 1999), Chap. 13, by permission of the author.

1 Corpora and language learning

> In this chapter you will get answers to the following questions:
>
> - What is a corpus?
> - Why use a corpus with language learners?
> - What are some ways to use a corpus with language learners?
> - What will corpus-based activities look like?

In recent years there has been an increased interest in corpus linguistics along with an increased interest in using corpora for language instruction. The goal of this book is to provide teachers and teachers-in-training with the background and information needed to use corpora for language teaching. You will learn how to use corpora as a resource for developing materials and activities for a variety of classroom language-teaching situations.

A different use of corpus linguistics, covered in other books, is to discover patterns of language use, which takes advanced research skills and often involves computational skills. This book will not explain the methods needed to carry out such corpus research but builds on that research. You will discover that it is relatively easy to use existing corpus-research findings and corpora to enhance your teaching. If you are interested in the research aspect of corpus linguistics, there are several books listed in Additional Reading at the end of this chapter which provide a solid introduction to corpus-linguistic research. In addition, there is an extensive list of both online and print resources provided in Appendix B.

Let's start by addressing some questions that will help to provide a foundation for the topics covered in the following chapters. These questions include:

- What is a corpus?
- Is one corpus as good as the next?
- Should I use a corpus to teach my students English?
- How can I use a corpus to teach my students English?

- How can I adapt and develop materials from corpora for use in my class-room?

A logical place to begin to answer these and other related questions is with an explanation and overview of what a corpus is.

What is a corpus?

In the world of corpus linguistics, a corpus is a large, principled collection of naturally occurring texts (written or spoken) stored electronically. Let's look more closely at this definition by answering the following questions: What is meant by "naturally occurring texts"? What about spoken language? What is "a principled collection"? How big is "large"?

What is meant by "naturally occurring texts"?

Naturally occurring texts is language that is from actual language situations, such as friends chatting, meetings, letters, class assignments, and books, rather than from surveys, questionnaires, or just made-up language.

What about spoken language?

Collecting a corpus of spoken language involves recording and then tran-scribing the spoken language. Creating written transcripts of spoken lan-guage can be quite time-consuming and involves a series of choices based on the interests of the corpus compilers. For example, if researchers are interested in how pauses are used, they may time the pauses between words and also between speaker turns. If this is not a primary concern of the researchers, then they may only note long pauses (e.g., those over five sec-onds) or not note any pauses. Transcribing a spoken corpus with prosodic information (rising and falling intonation) is a major undertaking and will often be accomplished in several stages. The first stage is a rough transcrip-tion; next the transcript is reviewed to mark the rising and falling patterns of the words. Even the supposedly simple task of just getting spoken words into written form requires several decisions. How will spoken contractions be transcribed? For example, if a speaker says, "Are you gonna call Sam tonight?" do you transcribe *gonna* as it was spoken (*gonna*), or as the con-ventional written version *going to*? Other examples include *kinda* instead of *kind of*, *gotta* instead of *got to*, and the reduced forms of *cuz* or *coz* for *because*. If you are interested in exploring whether these contracted or reduced forms have a pattern, or if they tend to occur with certain words and not others, then transcribing them true to the form uttered (e.g., writing *kinda* instead of *kind of*) would be essential.

Even with written texts, corpus compilers often have to make decisions about spelling conventions, punctuation, and errors such as word omissions or grammatical errors. The intended uses of the corpus shape the decisions made during the compilation of a corpus. For example, a corpus of essays written by language learners may prove a useful resource for teaching editing strategies. In this case, it would not be a good idea to correct spelling or other errors, since a class activity could involve editing the essays and discussing the types of changes that were made.

What is "a principled collection"?

The design of the corpus must be principled: The goals of the researcher or teacher shape the design of the corpus and guide the collection of texts. The texts in a corpus need to represent the type of language that the corpus is intending to capture. For example, if a corpus is to be representative of written language, then the corpus designer would need to make a comprehensive list of the different written language situations (e.g., fiction, academic prose, personal letters, office memos) and then create a plan to collect these various texts.

The task of collecting a general representative corpus is enormous. Fortunately, it is not necessary for interested teachers to build their own corpora. Several general corpora are readily available (see Appendix B), e.g., Brown; Lancaster, Oslo, Bergen corpus (LOB); British National Corpus (BNC); the Corpus of Contemporary American English (COCA), and the International Corpus of English (ICE), and provide valuable resources for information on how spoken and written language are used in a range of settings. However, in addition to corpora that represent written and spoken language in general, sometimes teachers need specialized corpora that represent a particular type of language use, such as EFL student compositions, university introductory chemistry lectures, lab reports, or business memos. Chapter 4 will provide some guidelines and ideas for how you can create your own specific corpora for classroom use.

How big is "large"?

In addition to being a principled collection of naturally occurring texts, another defining characteristic of a corpus is that it is a large collection of texts. However, *large* is an extremely relative term. As technology has advanced, corpus size has grown. In the 1960s, when some of the first electronic corpora were being built (e.g., LOB, Brown), one million words was considered large for a general corpus. Now, just over 40 years later, general corpora, the BNC for example, are often 100 million words, and COCA is over 400 million words! General corpora are often larger than specialized corpora since specialized corpora represent a smaller slice of language. So, although the notion of size is rather fluid, it is important to realize that size is a reflection of the type of corpus (general or specialized) and the purpose of the corpus. Though earlier corpora may seem small by today's standards, they continue to be used. Studies have shown that one million words is sufficient to obtain reliable, generalizable results for many, though not all, research questions (Biber 1993; Reppen & Simpson 2002). A one-million-word general corpus will be adequate to address linguistic patterns of use and grammatical co-occurrence patterns, but not for lexical investigations. For lexical investigations corpora need to be very large to ensure that all the senses of a word are represented.

Why use a corpus with language learners?

Corpus-based investigations can identify linguistic and situational co-occurrence patterns. Most fluent speakers of a language have strong and fairly accurate intuitions about whether a form is grammatical or not. For example, if you hear someone say, *He don't like apples*; you know that the correct form is *doesn't – He doesn't like apples*. However, when asked to comment on patterns of use (e.g., Which verb tense is most frequent in conversation? What are the 10 most frequent verbs in conversation?), native speakers' intuitions are often ill-informed (Biber & Reppen 2002). Native speakers often notice the marked, or unusual, rather than the unmarked, or typical, uses of language. It is in this area that corpus linguistics can make the greatest contribution to language teaching. Since corpus linguistics can provide descriptions of actual language use, this information can then be used to shape and develop language-teaching materials, and even be used to develop language tests.

English as a Second Language/Foreign Language (ESL/EFL) professionals, from teachers to testing specialists, repeatedly make decisions about language, including which linguistic features and vocabulary to teach and/or test. In recent years, most ESL/EFL professionals have adopted a preference for "authentic" materials, presenting language from natural texts rather than made-up examples (Byrd 1995; McDonough & Shaw 1993). Corpora provide a ready resource of natural, or authentic, texts for language learning. In addition to the preference for authentic texts, studies of second language learning have shown that when learners are engaged in meaningful activities (e.g., hands-on activities) that involve them in manipulating language, they learn more information and retain that information longer. Corpus activities directly address both of these areas by meaningfully engaging learners.

What are some ways to use a corpus with language learners?

There are several ways that corpora can be used in the classroom. These can range from focusing on individual linguistic features to focusing on characteristics of texts or varieties of language such as business memos, biology lab reports, campaign speeches, and the like. In the sections below, some of the various ways of using corpora are presented. Other tools and ways of looking at texts and linguistic features will be described in detail in the chapters that follow.

Using word lists

The corpus or corpora can be analyzed at several levels depending on the goals of the analyses. Vocabulary is usually a central concern in most language classrooms. Vocabulary provides the foundation to language learning, and this is an area where corpora can be a valuable language resource, in terms of both knowing what to teach and in providing a rich source of language practice. A useful tool for vocabulary learning is a concordance program. These programs can be used to generate word lists (for example, on the Web site Compleat Lexical Tutor, discussed in Chapter 3). In a reading class, for example, word lists can be used to identify words students will encounter in a reading. The teacher can then use the word lists to make certain the students control the vocabulary needed to read the text without too much difficulty.

Concordance programs create word lists that can be arranged in either alphabetical order or in order of word frequency (i.e., with the most frequent words appearing first). Knowing which words are infrequent in a text can also be important and give insight as to the specialized nature of the reading. Infrequent words most likely have specialized meanings that are specific to a particular area of study, which is especially true in scientific texts. Figure 1.1 shows a word frequency list from a subcorpus of 30 *New York Times* articles in the American National Corpus, generated using the concordance program MonoConc Pro 2.2 (Barlow 2002).

Count	Pct	Word
1455	**6.0491%**	**the**
666	2.7689%	to
651	2.7065%	a
594	2.4695%	and
480	1.9956%	of
462	1.9208%	in
239	0.9936%	for
211	0.8772%	said
207	0.8606%	that
199	0.8273%	he
197	0.8190%	was
196	0.8149%	with
169	0.7026%	is
163	0.6777%	it
158	0.6569%	on
158	0.6569%	his
154	0.6403%	by
140	0.5820%	as
130	0.5405%	but
119	0.4947%	who
112	0.4656%	at
110	0.4573%	be
101	0.4199%	have
95	0.3950%	had
95	0.3950%	i
93	0.3866%	are
93	0.3866%	not
89	0.3700%	from
84	0.3492%	–
84	0.3492%	this
81	0.3368%	they

MonoConc Pro – [Corpus Frequency List]
File Concordance Frequency Display Window Info

30 files in current corpus — 24,053 words, 5,110 types

Figure 1.1: A word frequency list in MonoConc Pro 2.2, from approx. 25,000 words from *New York Times* articles in the American National Corpus.

Table 1.1: *Frequency and alphabetical order word lists from 30* New York Times *articles (approx. 25,000 words) created using MonoConc Pro 2.2*

Frequency order		Alphabetical order	
frequency	word	frequency	word
1455	the	1	abandoned
666	to	1	abandonment
651	a	1	ability
594	and	3	able
480	of	1	abortion
462	in	56	about
239	for	2	absent
211	said	2	absolutely
207	that	1	absorbing
199	he	1	abundant
197	was	1	abusing
196	with	1	accept
169	is	1	accepted
163	it	1	access
158	on	1	accidental
158	his	1	accidents
154	by	1	acclimated
140	as	1	accolades
130	but	1	accompanied
119	who	8	according
112	at	2	accounting
110	be	1	accreditation
101	have	2	accused
95	had	2	accustomed
95	i	3	achieved
93	are	2	achievement

Table 1.1 shows the first 25 lines of the word list from this same small subcorpus of *New York Times* articles (approximately 25,000 words) in two different orders. The list on the left is in frequency order and the list on the right is in alphabetical order.

Your turn

Look at the word lists in Table 1.1 and think of two activities to do with students. Did you come up with any of the following ideas?

The information from the lists can be used as a starting point for several class activities:

- Discuss how the two lists are arranged (frequency vs. alphabetic). What are some of the differences in the types of words in the two lists?
- Find content words (i.e., nouns, adjectives, verbs, and adverbs) vs. function words (e.g., articles, pronouns, prepositions). Then answer the following questions: How many content words do you find in each list? How many function words? Why do you think there is a difference between the two lists?
- Find related word forms (*abandoned, abandonment; achieved, achievement*) and examine the role of prefixes and suffixes. How do prefixes or suffixes change the core meaning of a word? How do prefixes or suffixes change a word from a noun to a verb or vice versa?
- Explore which words in the alphabetical list can go with words in the frequency list (e.g., *ability to*), or use the words in the two lists as the basis for a sentence scramble activity.
- Ask students to scan the lists and mark unfamiliar words. Then use those words as a basis for a vocabulary lesson.

Even from something as simple as a word list, several meaningful learning activities can be developed.

Using concordance lines

As a learner, knowing which words go together – and which words do not go together – is often a puzzle. Teachers can spend many classroom hours trying to provide students with meaningful input on which words can go together and on how certain words occur in some situations of language use and not in others (e.g., chatting with friends vs. writing class papers). This is another area where using a corpus can provide valuable insights into patterns of use. In addition to generating word lists as shown above, a concordance program can be used to generate KWICs (Key Word In Context indexes). KWICs can provide information about the context of use for particular words or phrases. Figure 1.2 is a screen shot of concordance lines, or KWICs, generated by MonoConc Pro 2.2 for the target word *any*. As you can see in Figure 1.2, the word *any* in each piece of text is lined up in the middle of the display. The words that occur to the left and right of the target word are also displayed providing lots of information about the use of the target form *any* in context. The display can also be sorted in several ways, such as alphabetically by the words that occur immediately to

MonoConc Pro - [Concordance - [any]]

File Concordance Frequency Display Sort Window Info

<6> What was the score earlier when you last saw it?

<1> Four to three.

<6> Four to three. Yeah. Uh-huh.

<1> And the Twins won last night two to nothing.

<2> Isn't that strange? I could care a less. I don't have any interest whatsoever.

... again. <2> <-> <1> Need to find out if it's recording any. <2> How long are you supposed to be recording? ...
... any other reason+ <1> Yes. <2> + and+ <1> Do you watch any soaps anymore? <3> Yeah I watch two. <1> What do ...
... and the package stuff the sauces jams and any any kind of kitchen tool you want. Uh ...
... the package stuff the sauces jams and any any kind of kitchen tool you want. Uh Flagstaff ...
... Flagstaff needed something like that. We didn't have any thing. I've appreciated it. <2> I didn't <E> laughing <JE> <4> <-> no ...
... more vases. <E> laughing <JE> <2> I I don't think there's any question in my mind that I am winning. ...
...... come up with one that we figure is any better than the others. <4> Now do you not ...
...... fun to go there. Not professional entertainment by any means. <2> No. No. <4> College kids that are in ...
...... red hats on them. They can just be any kind of purple T-shirt and then some times ...
... pictures of the wedding because he wasn't getting any any from my sister who lives two miles ...
...... of the wedding because he wasn't getting any any from my sister who lives two miles away ...
...... upset about the whole thing. He wasn't getting any getting any pictures and he was checking with Patty and ...
... have some more pictures cause they'd never gotten any of the others. The day before or two ...
...... I was trying to see if I had any anywhere but I had gone ahead and printed ...
...... and she would sort them out not using any fancy words and <>. <5> <-> <E> laughing <JE> <3> <E> laughing <JE> <5
...... I love Manhattan clam chowder. <5> You can't it any place. <2> I just had clam chowder the other ...
... mother-in-law heard about <>. <-> clam chowder like that at any place. It just doesn't exist. And she kept ...
...... even have been this summer? And there weren't any good clams in the the stores so+ <4> Ah. ...
...... Okay. This is... This is+ <2> Do I get any points for that? <1> +chocolate pistachio bunt cake. You ...
...... go down after that. <3> Oh. <2> I didn't have any problems. I had chicken. <3> <E> laughing <JE> <4> This is not ...
...... was I was comfortable. I wasn't suffering in any way shape or form+ <4> Uh-huh. <2> + and this was ...
... cat if you <-> tin can. <2> He's never lived any place else and whether or not he would ...
... back. <2> <-> <2> Oh that was okay. I didn't book any trips back to Minneapolis <>. Boss said you got ...
... says Flagstaff call somebody. Hey are you having any meetings or anything? We were over at um ...
...... suitable and there was no thing wrong with any of those homes. Just <>. And they were two ...
... career that's <-> big promotion because I don't want any more. I just <>. It's funny too when I ...
...... and I think that moving from Minneapolis to any other city is what I was looking for. ...
...... ones are pretty sharp. Do you guys have any <>? Yeah. <M> <> <1> <> Yeah. <F> Good morning guys. <1> Hi. <F> Ho...

1319 matches   Original text order   Strings matching any

H:\Randall\Cambridge\CUP conversation corpus\t\0029001.txt   7.10 mbytes, 181 files

Figure 1.2: KWICs of the target word *any* in MonoConc Pro 2.2, from a corpus of spoken conversation.

9

the right or left of the target word. Some of the many ways to use KWICs will be discussed in more detail in Chapter 3.

The Sample Activity below is an example of how a teacher used information from corpus research and provided students with KWICs to help guide the students in learning the more frequent uses of the word *any*.

A corpus study by Mindt (1998) concluded that 50 percent of *any* use is in affirmative statements, 40 percent in negative statements, and only 10 percent in interrogatives. The exercise below uses 10 representative corpus examples. The purpose of this exercise is to get the students to discover use patterns and their relative frequency.

Sample Activity[1]

The word *any* is often taught in the following way:

> Interrogatives: Are there *any* Turkish students in your class?
> Negatives: No, there aren't *any* Turkish students in my class.
> Affirmatives: Yes, there are *any** Turkish students in my class.
>
> * Not grammatical

Part 1

Read through the following lines taken from a concordance of the word *any*.

- This is going to be a test like *any* other test, like, for example
- working with you. If there are *any* questions about how we're going to
- and I didn't receive *any* materials for the November meeting
- and it probably won't make *any* difference. I mean, that's the next
- You can do it *any* way you want.
- Do you want to ask *any* questions? Make any comments?
- I don't have *any* problem with that. I'm just saying
- if they make *any* changes, they would be minor changes.
- I think we ought to use *any* kind of calculator. I think that way
- I see it and it doesn't make *any* sense to me, but I can take that

What conclusions can you draw from these lines about the use of *any*?

Part 2

What are the three main uses of *any* in order of frequency?

An exercise like this would be part of a lesson in which the students were studying quantifiers or something related to quantifiers. The concordance

---

1. Adapted from iteslj.org/Articles/Krieger-Corpus.html

lines above can be exploited for other purposes as well, such as defining some of the functions of *any* and common language chunks that use *any*.

Your turn

Make a list of other words that you think might lend themselves to this type of guided discovery activity. Save your list so that you can use it to create some activities in Chapter 4.

OTHER WAYS TO USE CONCORDANCE LINES

Using concordance lines, teachers and researchers can also explore co-occurrence patterns. Certain lexical patterns and some basic grammatical patterns can be discovered through concordancing. Concordance output can also provide learners with information about word use and how the same word can sometimes have more than one meaning, as will be explored in several of the activities presented in later chapters.

Using tagged texts

One aspect that adds complexity to teaching a language is the fact that words can have different grammatical roles. For example the word *can* might be a noun referring to a *can of soda*, or it might be a modal expressing ability/possibility: *I can go with you*. Even in this case, a corpus can be a valuable resource for teachers. Some corpora are *tagged*, that is each word in the corpus is labeled for its part of speech or grammatical category (e.g., first person pronoun, verb, relative clause). The process of creating a tagged corpus is quite sophisticated and is beyond the scope of this book as it requires computer programming skills. Although developing and processing a corpus for tagging requires sophisticated skills, using tagged corpora does not require sophisticated programming skills and can provide useful information to the user.

Text Sample 1 on p. 12 is an excerpt from a tagged text. The sentence, "I'm gonna ask you to pay sixty or seventy dollars for a textbook." has been tagged using a tagger developed by Doug Biber (for more information see Biber 1988; Conrad and Biber 2001). The labels in the right-hand column do not appear in the program but were added here to make the tag codes clearer. Although this particular example uses Biber's tagger, the codes are similar to those found in other tagging programs. Appendix B lists some resources for tagging texts.

Text sample 1: Example of tagged text

Word	Tag	Label
I	^pp1a+pp1+++	first person pronoun
'm	^vb+bem+aux++0	BE verb, auxiliary, contracted form
gonna	^md+prd+++0	modal, contracted form
ask	^vb++++	base verb
you	^pp2+pp2+++	second person pronoun
to	^to++++	to clause
pay	^vbi++++	infinitive form of verb
sixty	^cd++++	cardinal number
or	^cc++++	coordinating conjunction
seventy	^cd++++	cardinal number
dollars	^nns++++	noun – plural
for	^in++++	preposition
a	^at++++	article
textbook	^nn++++	noun – singular
.	^.+clp+++	end punctuation

By using texts that have been tagged, teachers can answer a range of different types of questions. For example, we can see what grammatical structures tend to co-occur, such as which verbs most frequently take complement clauses (e.g., I think that..., I know that...). Tagged texts are also very useful when dealing with words that have multiple functions, such as *well,* which can be a noun, verb, adjective, adverb, interjection, or discourse marker. Teachers and students can use tagged texts to search and create lists of nouns or prepositions that occur in a text and then look at these in context to get a clear sense of the meaning. In Chapter 3 we will explore some of the ways that tagged texts can be used in the classroom.

The role of register

Language teachers are often concerned with the different contexts of language use and helping learners understand how language can vary depending on these different contexts. Corpora can be a valuable teacher resource for creating activities that help learners understand variation due to situational factors, or register. *Register* is a term used to describe varieties of texts that are defined by situational characteristics (e.g., spoken vs. written, edited vs. real-time). The term *register* can be used at various levels of specificity. For example, spoken language vs. written language would be a broad register distinction. The register of spoken language could be further subdivided into the registers of face-to-face conversations and phone

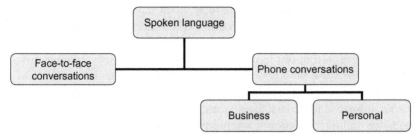

Figure 1.3: Some of the subregisters of spoken language.

conversations; the subregister of phone conversations could then be further divided into business vs. personal phone conversations, as illustrated in Figure 1.3.

The situational characteristics of language use, or register, has a strong impact on the linguistic features associated with that register. Each register has its own unique linguistic patterns. For example, one of the features associated with face-to-face conversations is repetition (e.g., "I bet I . . . I bet I, I put an *s* on it"). This type of repetition is likely due to the speaker producing spoken language under real-time constraints. This type of repetition is seldom found in written language since writers usually have time to produce language and do not need to "buy time" to think of a word while maintaining their position as a speaker in the conversation.

When using a corpus for instructional purposes it is important that the corpus represent the register that is being taught. For example, we would not want to use a corpus of informal conversation as a basis for academic writing instruction, or vice versa.

Your turn

Think about the classes that you plan to teach. Make a list of each register that you are planning to teach your students (e.g., business English, conversational English, medical English). Now make another list of the different situations that can occur within those registers (e.g., phone conversations, memo writing, note taking). What kinds of authentic texts, or corpora, would you want available to teach your classes? Keep this list, so that in Chapter 4 you can create materials based on your needs.

What will corpus-based materials look like?

Some activities that are corpus-informed, such as those using concordance lines, might look different than traditional textbook exercises; however many of the activities and formats look much like non-corpus–informed activities. It is the content that will differ. The order of information presentation may also differ. For example, in a beginning conversation class the verbs that are introduced in corpus-informed material may contain irregular verbs because we know from corpus research that the verbs, *think, have, go,* and *come,* are extremely frequent in conversation. Therefore, in corpus-informed materials, these verbs would be presented early on, unlike the more traditional approach where irregular verbs are kept for later units. Although the activities shown in Figure 1.4 may look similar to those found in many ESL/EFL textbooks, the content being presented is not typical since it introduces an irregular verb at a very early stage, in the third unit in this case. These activities also reflect some of the many different meanings of the verb *have.*

The example in Figure 1.4 is a nice example of how corpus linguistics can be used to inform instruction and materials development, and yet retain the familiar appearance that learners and teachers are accustomed to, thus not scaring anyone away from the material being presented.

To see an example of a corpus-informed course book with an integrated-skills focus that goes beyond vocabulary, let's look at Figure 1.5, an excerpt from *Touchstone,* a four-level, corpus-informed series for English language instruction. You will notice that the activities look very similar to those found in a traditional course book. The content, however, is not the same. Take a look at the conversation in Section 3. When you hear or read this conversation, it feels genuine, not like a made-up textbook conversation. It is a real conversation. It has pauses and fillers (e.g., *uh*). Traditional textbooks usually do not include these valuable and typical features of conversation, yet fluent speakers regularly use pauses and fillers as they think about what they are going to say. It seems that if a feature is very common, and is used by fluent native speakers of a language, then we should certainly teach that feature to learners. Using corpora allows us to identify these features, and corpus-informed materials help us present them to our students.

Looking at Section 4 in the *Touchstone* example in Figure 1.5, note the *In conversation . . .* box. This box contains information about language use based on a spoken corpus, letting students know which forms are most frequent in conversation. Only corpus-informed books can provide students with this type of information. Sometimes, traditional textbooks attempt to provide this information, however, but because it is based on intuition rather than on actual language use, such information presented is often incorrect.

In addition to these types of materials, there are now several ESL/EFL textbooks that use the Academic Word List (Coxhead 2000) to provide teachers and students with ready-made, corpus-informed material for vocabulary instruction.

Exercises

3.1 Fill in the blanks. Use words from B, C, and D on page 6.

1. I never have a big ....*breakfast*... in the morning.
2. I have an .... with the doctor at 1 o'clock.
3. I had a .... yesterday, so I studied all night.
4. Mike is having a .... on Saturday night. Are you going?
5. I'm too busy, so I don't have .... to take a vacation.
6. I have a terrible .... I keep sneezing. Atchoo!
7. I had a .... with Maria last night. We went out to dinner and a movie.
8. Keiko is going to have a .... She thinks it'll be a girl.

3.2 Answer these questions about *yourself.*

1. Do you have any brothers or sisters? If yes, how many?
2. Which days do you have classes?
3. What do you usually have for lunch?
4. On weekends do you have to get up early in the morning?
5. Do you have coffee or tea with breakfast?
6. Is there anything you don't have at home that you want to have? What is it?
7. Do you ever have trouble understanding English? When?
8. Do you have to study hard to learn English? Why?

3.3 Do the crossword puzzle.

Across
1. You can have one in a restaurant.
3. Some people like to have one on New Year's Eve.
5. You have this between meals.

Down
2. You have these at school.
4. If you don't want coffee, you can have ....

3.4 Complete the sentences using *have.*

1. A: I'm thirsty!
   B: Why don't you .... ?
2. A: I feel sick today.
   B: Do you .... ?
3. A: Bye, everyone! I'm leaving for my trip to Hawaii!
   B: Bye .... !
4. A: Can you come to my party on Friday?
   B: I can't, I have a big test on Monday and I .... this weekend.

Figure 1.4: An example of a corpus-informed vocabulary book. The corpus was used to determine the order of the information presented in the vocabulary units. (*Basic Vocabulary in Use*, McCarthy & O'Dell 2010, p. 7)

3 Building language

A 🎧 Listen. What does Carla think of the band? Practice the conversation.

Alex Listen. What do you think of this song?

Carla It's good – I like it. Who is it?

Alex A new band . . . some local guys. Do you like them?

Carla They're local? Really? They're pretty good. Who's the
lead singer? I like her. She sounds like Mariah Carey.

Alex Yeah, everybody says that. It's my friend Lori.

Carla Who's the guy singing with her? I'm not sure about him.

Alex Uh . . . actually, that's me. I'm in the band, too.

Figure
it out ▸ **B** Complete the conversations. Then ask a partner your
questions. Give your own answers.

❶ *A* What do you think of _____ (male singer)?
 B I like _____ .

❷ *A* Do you know _____ (female singer)?
 B No, I don't know _____ .

4 Grammar *Object pronouns; everybody, nobody* 🎧

I'm a singer. That's **me** on the CD.	It's a nice song. I like **it**.	Everybody
You're a musician? I'd like to hear **you**.	We play in a band. Come listen to **us**.	Everyone
She's pretty good. I like **her**.	**They**'re local guys. Do you like **them**?	Nobody
He's not a good singer. I don't like **him**.		No one

Everybody / Everyone / Nobody / No one ┤ likes pop.

A Complete the questions with object pronouns. Complete the
answers with *everybody* or *nobody*. Then practice with a partner.

In conversation . . .

Everybody and *nobody*
are more common than
everyone and *no one*.

1. *A* I listen to hip-hop a lot. Do you listen to __it__ , too?
 B Yes. __Everybody__ in my school listens to hip-hop.

2. *A* Ricky Martin – he was on TV last night. Do you know _____ ?
 B Of course I do. _____ knows Ricky Martin.

3. *A* I don't really like classical music. Do you ever listen to _____ ?
 B Yes, but with earphones – _____ in my family likes it.

4. *A* I like Alicia Keys. She's a good singer. What do you think of _____ ?
 B Oh, almost _____ is a fan of Alicia Keys.

5. *A* My favorite band is Coldplay. I think they're great. Do you like _____ ?
 B Yeah. They're the best. _____ plays rock like they do.

	everybody
	everyone
	nobody
	no one

Figure 1.5: An example of corpus-based information presented in a format
similar to traditional course books (*Touchstone* Level 2, McCarthy, McCarten,
& Sandiford 2004, p. 15).

Although corpus-informed textbooks are still relatively new, most learners and teachers are familiar with the corpus-based ESL/EFL dictionaries
that are available, such as the *Cambridge Dictionary of American English*
and *Longman's Dictionary of Contemporary English* or the *Cambridge*

Academic Content Dictionary, which additionally incorporates the vocabulary of the Academic Word List. These dictionaries provide learners with important information about contexts of use and also nuances of meaning that are not commonly found in first language dictionaries since most native speakers have control of these subtle meaning differences.

Your turn

Pick a corpus-based and a non-corpus-based dictionary. Think of two or three words and look them up in each of the dictionaries. Compare the dictionary entries. Are the definitions the same? Does the information presented differ? If so, how does it differ? Does one type of dictionary provide more information about actual use?

Putting it all together

As we see in this chapter, information from corpus linguistics can be used to inform language teaching in several ways ranging from helping teachers decide course content or informing the order of presenting information to having learners actually interact with corpora. Corpora that represent the types of language, or registers, that are being taught can be a useful tool for teachers and students. And equally important, although the area of corpus linguistics is complex, the task of using corpora or information from corpus research in the language classroom does not have to be overwhelming. The next three chapters will provide information and detailed examples of how to use information from corpus research to inform teaching decisions and step-by-step instructions for how to use corpus resources for language instruction.

Additional reading

Aston, G., Bernardini, S., & Stewart, D. (2005). *Corpora and language learners*. Amsterdam: John Benjamins.

Baker, P., Hardie, A., & McEnery, T. (2006). *A glossary of corpus linguistics*. Edinburgh: Edinburgh Press.

Biber, D. (2006). *University language: A corpus-based study of spoken and written registers*. Amsterdam: John Benjamins.

Biber, D., Conrad, S., & Reppen, R. (1998). *Corpus linguistics: Exploring language structure and use*. Cambridge: Cambridge University Press.

Coxhead, A. (2000). A new academic word list. *TESOL Quarterly* 34:213–38.

Gavioli, L. (2001). The learner as researcher: Introducing corpus concordancing in the classroom. In G. Aston (ed.), *Learning with corpora* (pp. 108–37). Houston, TX: Athelstan.

Gavioli, L., & Aston, G. (2001). Enriching reality: Language corpora in language pedagogy. *ELT Journal* 55:238–46.

Kennedy, G. (1998). *An introduction to corpus linguistics*. London: Longman.

McEnery, T., & Wilson, A. (1996). *Corpus linguistics*. Edinburgh: Edinburgh University Press.

Meyer, C. (2002). *English corpus linguistics*. Cambridge: Cambridge University Press.

O'Keefe, A., McCarthy, M., & Carter, R. (2007). *From corpus to classroom*. Cambridge: Cambridge University Press.

Reppen, R., & Simpson, R. (2002). Corpus linguistics. In N. Schmitt (ed.), *An introduction to applied linguistics* (pp. 92–111). London: Arnold.

Sinclair, J. (Ed.). (2004). *How to use corpora in language teaching*. Amsterdam: John Benjamins.

2 Using corpus studies to inform language teaching

In this chapter you will get answers to the following questions:

• What corpus-based teaching materials are available?

• How can I develop materials and activities based on corpus research?

This chapter will provide information about corpus-based resources that can be used for teaching. Two types of material will be presented: teaching materials that have been developed based on corpus research; and information and guidelines to develop materials and activities based on corpus findings. This chapter will show how to take information from corpus-based research studies and convert that information into usable classroom material and activities.

What corpus-based materials are available?

As mentioned in Chapter 1, for many years ESL/EFL dictionaries have been based on information from corpora. In addition to more accurate definitions, these dictionaries include information about how words are used; for example, some words tend to be used mostly in spoken rather than written language. Learner dictionaries provide powerful tools for students and have become the norm in most ESL/EFL classrooms. Dictionaries that are written for native English speakers often begin with definitions that may not reflect actual use patterns. It is even more difficult for the definition to capture the semantic prosody, or flavor of the word. The Your Turn activity below provides a nice example of this point.

Your turn

Use two dictionaries: one ESL/EFL learner dictionary that is corpus based and a dictionary for native English-speakers that is not corpus based (most native-speaker dictionaries are not corpus based). Look up the verb *commit* and write down the first two definitions. Are they the same or different? Which of the dictionaries best captures the meaning of *commit* as it is most often used? How could this information be of use to your students?

In the native-speaker dictionary, the first definition of *commit* probably focused on the notion of promise or obligation whereas the learner dictionary's first definition probably focused on doing something wrong, as in some sort of crime. This information about the "flavor" of a word is very helpful to language learners. This is also exactly the kind of information that can only be revealed through the use of corpora in dictionary compilation. Using corpus-based learner dictionaries in the classroom can be a rich and easily accessible source of activities.

In recent years the increased awareness of the benefits of using language-teaching material that is based on corpus linguistic research can be seen in the flurry of vocabulary books based on the Academic Word List (Coxhead 2000). These vocabulary books use information from Averil Coxhead's research on a 3.5-million-word corpus of written academic language covering a range of different disciplines. There are several books now on the market that are based on the information from the Academic Word List. A list of these books is provided at the end of this chapter.

In addition to using corpora to help create reference works and materials for vocabulary teaching, publishers are now using corpora to inform course books. For example, *Touchstone* (McCarthy, McCarten, & Sandiford 2004) is a four-level integrated-skills series that uses material that has been informed by corpus research. Throughout each lesson the student sees information panels or highlighted information from corpus research about actual language use. Some examples include panels with words that frequently occur together, or collocate; panels with words that are used most often in conversation when something goes wrong, such as *ooh*, *uh-oh*, and *oops*; and information about grammar structures, along with information about how these structures are used in different contexts. This information is very useful to language learners and teachers and is made readily accessible.

Corpus-informed teaching materials provide students with examples of real language use, helping learners to know how to use language that is appropriate in different contexts. As more and more material that is corpus-informed becomes available, language teachers can use these materials to provide learners with information that will help them achieve goals of language fluency. Corpus-informed materials also help hone our teaching by allowing us to have ready access to contextualized examples of language use and information about how language varies in different situations; rather than having to come up with material that contextualizes language use that addresses a range of situations, teachers can use corpus examples.

There are also several Web sites that provide materials and lessons for language instruction that are a result of corpus research. For example, the Web site of the Michigan Corpus of Academic Spoken English (MICASE) has a number of teaching activities that can be used in preparing students who will be studying in a university English-speaking setting. In Chapter 3 and in Appendix B we will take a look at the resources that are available on the Web, including a closer look at the resources available from the MICASE site.

How can I develop materials and activities using corpus research?

Now that you have an idea of how corpus research can be a useful tool for creating teaching materials, you will want to know how to find information from corpus research and use that to inform what you teach and to develop activities. Fortunately there are some easily accessible resources to help with course planning and materials development.

A starting point

The ideas and approaches used to select materials and create activities that are described in this chapter can be applied to a number of different contexts. Because there is such a wide range of goals for learning English and an equally vast range of contexts where English is taught, for the purpose of this section, the focus will be on adult ESL/EFL instruction that has the goal of preparing students to enroll in universities where English is spoken, or English for Academic Purposes (EAP). The principles and processes for making choices about how to select a feature is similar across the different contexts of instruction. So, as you look at the information presented in this section, think about how you can apply it to your particular context. Knowing which words or grammatical features are typical for particular contexts of language use is a good starting point for instruction, and the resources presented will provide information that is relevant for several contexts.

There are three resources that will be used in this section to provide information about university language. The first two are books based on the

TOEFL 2000 Corpus of Spoken and Written Academic Language (T2K-SWAL): *Representing Language Use in the University: Analysis of the TOEFL 2000 Spoken and Written Academic Language Corpus*[1] (Biber et al. 2004); and *University Language: A Corpus-based Study of Spoken and Written Registers* (Biber 2006). The third resource is the *Longman Grammar of Spoken and Written English* (Biber et al. 1999). A quick glance at any of these books highlights the tremendous vocabulary load of written academic English. Because of the important role vocabulary plays in academic English, we will begin by looking at some materials and activities that can be developed to help increase students' vocabulary.

In Appendix A you will find some lists and information that we will use throughout as a basis for different activities. Sometimes portions of the lists will be presented in the chapters, but other times you will be asked to go to the appendix to work with the material.

As you recall from Chapter 1, corpus-based activities do not necessarily look different from the activities and exercises that we are accustomed to; the difference is in the content that is presented, not necessarily in the format of the activity. So, with that in mind, let's get started.

Creating an activity to boost academic reading vocabulary

Before we can create an activity, we need a context or a learning goal. Teachers do not just create activities for the sake of creating activities. The context for this example will be a reading class. In academic classes, reading plays a central role in gaining information, and learners are often expected to read material and then to be able to write or speak about the material. From research, we know that to read a text successfully you need to know about 97 percent of the words in the text (Nation 2007; Schmitt 2008). We also know from reading research that reading fluency and vocabulary are closely related and have a cyclical relationship. The more you read, the more vocabulary you learn; and the more vocabulary you know, the easier it is to read (Grabe & Stoller 2001; Grabe 2009). This information about the demands of academic reading reinforces the key role that vocabulary instruction should have in teaching academic English. Corpus research can play a vital role to insure that we are teaching the words that our students will need. So, how will we develop materials from corpus research? In the following example, the steps for creating a vocabulary activity are outlined to demonstrate how to move from corpus information to classroom activity.

1. This is available online at www.ets.org/research/researcher/RM-04-03.html.

Although the steps are based on an example for a reading class, the process is similar regardless of the teaching context.

STEPS FOR CREATING A CORPUS-BASED VOCABULARY ACTIVITY

1. What do we know about the linguistic characteristics of academic texts?

From corpus research, we know that academic reading relies heavily on nouns. From corpus studies of academic texts we know that the ratio of nouns to verbs is heavily tipped toward nouns. In contrast, we find that in spoken language, conversation, and even academic lectures, the use of nouns and verbs is fairly evenly distributed (Biber 2006).

2. How can we use this information about academic texts to shape vocabulary instruction?

A teacher preparing students to meet the demands of university classes can use this information to design vocabulary material that would help students be better prepared to meet the demands of academic reading. To begin with, the vocabulary instruction would emphasize learning nouns, not to the exclusion of learning verbs, but the instruction would certainly focus on the acquisition of nouns and look at how nouns are formed. We know that two major ways that nouns are formed are through compounding and by the addition of affixes (that is, prefixes or suffixes).

3. What do we know from corpus research about the usefulness of affixes?

From corpus research (Biber et al. 1999) we learn that suffixes are much more productive than prefixes, and that not all suffixes are equally productive when it comes to academic words. That is to say, that there are some suffixes that are used much more often. The six most productive suffixes used with academic words are: *-tion, -ity, -er, -ness, -ism,* and *-ment.*

Knowing the answers to the questions posed in these steps gives us a foundation for creating teaching material. The information presented was easily obtained from existing and readily available resources. Now, we can now go about designing activities that use the six most productive suffixes as a basis for some vocabulary-building activities. Here are two examples of activities that could be created based on this information:

One very simple activity might be to give students some pages of academic text, perhaps a copy of a page from a textbook or a journal article in the case of graduate students. Ask the students to circle all of the nouns that they find with any of the six suffixes listed above. Then as a class there could be a discussion about these words, including looking at which words were nouns or verbs before the suffixes were added (e.g., *paint* → *painter* = verb → noun or noun → noun, depending on the context; *govern* → *government* = verb → noun).

A second activity might involve a matching, with nouns or verbs in one column and the suffixes in another. Students would match verbs or nouns with the suffixes and then use them in sentences. Or this could be presented as a fill-in-the-blank activity for a lower level. An example of this type is presented in the following Sample Activity. Of course, the real activity would have more words to work with and more sentences.

Sample Activity
Match the words on the left with suffixes on the right. Remember that some words might go with more than one suffix.

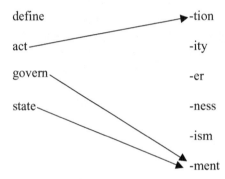

define   -tion

act   -ity

govern   -er

state   -ness

        -ism

        -ment

Use the new words you made to complete the sentences below.

1. The mayor made a _____ that upset the voters.
2. The _____ has raised taxes.
3. This _____ caused the people to revolt.

Your turn

Reflect on the process used to create the activities described. How could you adapt this process to be useful in your teaching context? List the changes that you would need to make. How are your changes influenced by your teaching context?

This process can also be a stepping-stone to other activities, such as discussing spelling changes and rules (*act* + *tion* = *action*, not *acttion*), or how verbs can be changed to nouns but still, in most cases, retain much of their central meanings.

As can be seen from the steps taken to create this activity, it would not take a lot of time or research; it's just a matter of taking existing corpus research and transforming it into practical classroom activities that reinforce the learning goals, in this case using corpus research to help boost academic vocabulary for reading.

Going beyond a word

Building vocabulary is an important goal for any language classroom. But learning one word at a time will make acquiring the vocabulary needed for academic contexts an enormous task. So, how can we use information from corpus research to take us beyond the level of the word? Certainly it must be more efficient to learn groups or chunks of language rather than just always learning words in isolation (Schmitt 2004).

Anyone who has traveled to a country where you do not know the language has probably relied on a language phrase book. These small, pocket-size books often have phrases such as *Where is the . . . . ?* and *How much does . . . . cost?* with each question followed by a list of useful nouns that can be used to fill the blank. It can be seen in these language phrase books there are groups of words that are very useful to learn. Corpus linguistics has also identified groups of words that commonly go together. These words that tend to co-occur are called collocates. When there are several words that tend to occur together, say a group of three, four, or five words that often are found together, these are called lexical bundles, or chunks, or formulaic sequences. These different terms have some technical differences that are of interest to applied linguists but are not relevant to the point that is being made here. If you are interested in learning more about this, articles and books on this topic are listed in Additional Reading at the end of this chapter.

So, in keeping with our theme of an academic English setting, we will use the resources from Appendix A of the T2K-SWAL book (Biber et al. 2004). Table 2.1 on page 26 lists four-word noun, prepositional, or verb phrase lexical bundles that typically occur, sorted by the lexical bundles found most frequently in classroom teaching, and those most common in textbooks. Lexical bundles with nouns and prepositional phrases were selected for this activity because of the major role these forms play in academic language (Biber et al. 1999).

One very quick and easy activity is to simply look at the distribution of bundles across the two contexts in Table 2.1 – textbooks and classroom

Table 2.1: *The distribution of lexical bundles by type and context for four-word bundles that occur more than 40 times per million words*

	Classroom teaching	Textbooks
Noun or prepositional phrase	a lot of people a lot of the a lot of times	as a result of in the form of in the United States on the basis of the nature of the the size of the
Verb phrase	going to be a going to have to have a lot of how many of you I'm not going to I don't know how I want to do is going to be let us talk about take a look at we're going to have what I want to you don't want to you know I mean you know if you you look at the	can be used to

teaching – and note the difference between the types of bundles that occur in classroom teaching versus textbooks. Immediately a pattern of use is apparent. Classroom language uses a much greater variety of verb bundles than the textbooks, while the textbooks use more prepositional or noun bundles.

Your turn

Look at the bundles listed in Table 2.1 and think of how you can use this information to create a classroom activity for your students. Jot down your ideas before reading the activities below.

Sample Activity

Using Table 2.1, ask each student to pick five lexical bundles found in classroom teaching. Then ask students either to listen to an academic lecture online or visit an academic class and note each time the bundles that they selected were used. An easy way to do this is to create a table with the bundle on the left and a space to place marks for

Ali's bundle list

Lexical bundle	Times used in class
we're going to have	||||
let us talk about	||
take a look at	||||||||||||
I want to do	
you know if you	

Figure 2.1: An example of a student's research results

counting on the right. See the example in Figure 2.1. When the students return to the language classroom from this action research, compile a list of the bundles that were used and look at the range of frequency of use from the different classroom visits.

Sample Activity

After seeing the distribution of bundles from the students' class visits, a good follow-up activity is to look at the different purposes the bundles perform. Some bundles are clearly providing a macro structure for class expectations, such as *you know if you*; *you look at the*; and *how many of you*. If you have access to the Web in your classroom or a computer lab, you could look up these classroom verb bundles in the lectures that are available online from the MICASE site (more on this in Chapter 3). Once students have looked at KWICs from the MICASE site, answer the following question: What do the contexts of use for these classroom bundles look like? Students could be divided into teams to look up sets of bundles and then report on their use. If the MICASE site is not available, another option is to have students revisit classes where they collected bundle counts and do targeted listening for two specific bundles, paying close attention to when and how the bundles are used. Then the students can compare their results when they are back in the language classroom.

These two sample activities serve to raise awareness through focused listening. A greater awareness of the differences in what students encounter when listening to lectures versus reading textbooks will better prepare them for the demands of academic classes. These activities also raise awareness of the functions that these chunks of language can have.

The context of language use

One of the principle hurdles that students face is learning which forms of language to use in which contexts. Often, students who learned English in a setting that emphasized either literate skills or oral/aural aspects are uncertain of how to use language in a context that requires the use of the nonemphasized skill. For example, if a student was responsible for reading and writing English but never had many opportunities to interact with native English-speakers, his or her spoken English may sound very booklike when using the language for informal conversation. Or, students who have been using spoken English mostly in informal contexts may not realize that they cannot use those same forms when writing academic essays, or even in class presentations. These situations relate back to the notion of register presented in the previous chapter.

For us as teachers, corpus linguistics can also provide support for instruction in this area. By consulting resources such as the *Longman Grammar of Spoken and Written English* (LGSWE) (Biber et al. 1999), teachers can easily get information that can be useful in shaping instruction. Because the LGSWE provides detailed comparisons of four registers of language use, teachers can see how different structures and even vocabulary varies across these different contexts of use. The four registers that are used in the LGSWE are fiction, newspaper, conversation, and academic prose. The last two registers – conversation and academic prose – can very productively be compared to raise awareness of language forms that are central to these contexts of language use. This information can also help to determine which forms teachers spend valuable class time on.

For example, many second language learners struggle with prepositions, in particular with knowing which prepositions to use when. How can we use LGSWE to shed light on this struggle? Well, we know that passives are often a feature in the context of academic writing. So, we can look in the LGSWE and see which verbs frequently occur in the passive and if these verbs have any preferences for occurring with particular prepositions. In LGSWE (p. 479), we find a list of 14 verbs that occur in the passive over 90 percent of the time in academic prose. We can also see that five of these verbs have very strong associations with particular prepositions. Using this information, we can teach students which verbs frequently are used in the passive and also which prepositions will tend to occur with which verbs, thus helping narrow the possibility for errors. The five verb + preposition associations that frequently occur together are: *aligned with*; *based on*; *coupled with*; *attributed to*; and *subjected to*.

This is just one example of the lists based on corpus data that can be found and easily translated into useful teaching information. As you can see, this was not a difficult task and did not require hours of research. It simply involved looking up some information and then making a list. Obviously there are many options for how such information can then be used in teaching. One way is to simply present the information in list form to learners as a resource. Other options include matching or fill-in-the-blank activities. Another activity could involve looking in textbooks or academic journals and finding these verb + preposition combinations in context.

Putting it all together

This chapter has focused on using existing corpus resources and showing how the information can then be applied to create activities that can be used in almost any classroom. While in some cases the steps used to create the activities presented in this chapter are not always explicitly stated, by looking over the example activities we see the process of creating activities or teaching material from corpus research can be summarized in these three questions:

1. What language feature or context of language use do I want to teach?
2. What can corpus research tell me about this feature, or context of language use?
3. How can I use this information to create meaningful activities for my students?

By using these three questions as a starting point, teachers can create materials for teaching a range of different language features or to address a variety of different contexts of language use.

In these first two chapters, there has not been any use of the computer for exploring corpora or creating materials. So far, the reader has been asked only to look at existing information and then use that information to inform teaching. In the next chapter we will use computers to explore how corpora can be used in the language classroom and will look at using online resources for both teachers and students. Chapter 4 will present ideas for using corpora in the classroom for hands-on learning and discuss how to create corpora for classroom use.

Additional reading

A sample of books based on the Academic Word List

Huntley, H. (2006). *Essential academic vocabulary*. Boston: Houghton Mifflin Co.
Schmitt, D., & Schmitt, N. (2005). *Focus on vocabulary*. New York: Longman.

Articles and books related to fixed expressions, lexical bundles, and formulaic sequences

Although by no means exhaustive, here is a starting point for those who are interested in reading more about groups of words that co-occur and some of the research that has been done in this area.

Biber, D., Conrad, S., & Cortes, V. (2004). If you look at . . . : Lexical bundles in university teaching and textbooks. *Applied Linguistics*, 25 (3), 371–405.

Moon, R. (1998). *Fixed expressions and idioms in English: A corpus-based approach*. Oxford: Oxford University Press.

Schmitt, N. (Ed.) (2004). *Formulaic sequences*. Amsterdam: John Benjamins.

3 Using corpus Internet resources in the classroom

In this chapter you will get answers to the following questions:

- How can I evaluate online corpus resources?
- What corpus teaching resources are available online?
- What corpora are available online?
- How can I use online corpora with my students?

The focus in this chapter is on resources that are available online. These resources include Web sites that range from interfaces with corpora to sites having teaching materials based on corpus findings. Because Web site addresses change, and some sites go out of existence, I will refer only to sites that are reliable and that should remain stable. These sites are listed in Appendix B. In addition, the companion Web site to this book lists additional online resources and attempts to keep the Web links up-to-date. There is a plethora of available Web sites that will not be covered in this chapter or in the appendix. Many of these may be useful to your particular teaching situation, which is why this chapter provides some guidelines that can help you evaluate other online corpus resources that you come across.

The list of Web sites in Appendix B is a good starting point for discovering some of the types of online resources that are available. More detailed information about some of those sites, along with details for activities and ideas for using these sites as resources for instruction are given in the following sections. The *Using Corpora in the Language Classroom* companion Web site includes a PowerPoint presentation with detailed instructions for working with two of the sites described below and lesson plans using online resources.

Evaluating online resources

As with all online resources, it is important to be aware of the variation in quality that can exist. With so many new sites appearing daily, it is essential to establish your guidelines for evaluating them. These guidelines should include considering who created the site, for what purpose, and how that purpose matches your intended uses. There might be an amazing site that has hundreds of scripts from TV dialogues, but if your goal is academic writing instruction, the site with TV scripts will not be a useful resource. Defining your goals for using a site, or any other resource for that matter, is probably the most important factor in evaluating any Web resource.

The site's integrity is another factor. One indication of a site's integrity is if it has been referenced in reputable publications, or if the site has a history of being cited by others as a resource; then it may be a useful resource. Most professional journals for language teaching and TESOL have a section that discusses online resources, and these often contain reviews of Web sites. Now, with the increased popularity of using corpus resources, many of these reviews and discussions include corpus-based Web sites.

Before you begin to look for online corpus resources, use these questions to help you consider some factors that can inform your choices:

1. Is the site for me, or is it for my students?
2. What do I want to use the site for? Do I want to find out about a particular language feature and then use that information to develop materials or an activity? Do I want my students to use the site? If so, do I want them to use it during lab time or on their own?
3. Do I want a site with prepared activities or materials?

Your turn

List two or three areas of language (e.g., business English, vocabulary) that you would like to find corpus resources for. Or, use the list you created in Chapter 1. Try to find one or two Web sites that have corpus resources related to your interests, then use the following checklist to evaluate the sites you found. Be sure to be explicit when answering the questions. It might be useful to write out the answers to the questions.

Let's say that you found a few sites that you would like to evaluate. One of them is a little-known site, and you are not sure if it is a useful resource. Of course, your specific goals for use will be the main criteria that you will use to determine if the site meets your needs. Here is a checklist that can be used to help evaluate the usefulness of online resources.

Site evaluation checklist
- How do I want to use this site?
- Does the site match my purposes/goals?

- Does the site do what it says it will do?
- Is the site stable, or does it crash/freeze my computer?
- Are the instructions clear and easy to follow? (This is particularly relevant if learners will be using the site.)
- Is there is a user fee? Does the fee match the use that I anticipate? In other words, is this a good value?

As you begin to discover sites, you will fine-tune your sense for judging the usefulness of a particular Web site. You should add to or modify the checklist with ideas of your own.

Using available resources

It's time to explore some sites that have premade corpus-based resources. As mentioned earlier, these include both teacher and student online corpus-based resources. First, we will look at the resources that are available for teachers. Then, we will look at sites that have activities for students. Of course the student sites can also be a resource for teachers.

Teacher resources

We will look at two types of corpus-based teacher resources that are available online. The first type provides information that can be used to inform instruction or that can be used as a starting point for materials development related to a particular language point (as was described in Chapter 2). For example, perhaps a particular language point has come up in class and you would like more information to be able to develop an activity to help your students better understand that language point, or to have additional practice with a particular language feature. The second type provides actual corpus-based lesson plans.

Let's look at two resources that can provide teachers with information about particular aspects of language use: the Kibbitzer pages developed by Tim Johns,[1] and the MICASE Kibbitzer.[2] Both of these sites use corpus-based research to provide information for teachers and for advanced language learners to use to help inform their language choices. Both sites often use the format of providing KWICs to expose the user to a large number of examples of the target form.

1. www.eisu.bham.ac.uk/support/online/kibbitzers.shtml
2. micase.elicorpora.info/micase-kibbitzers

We will begin by looking at the classic Kibbitzer pages at the University of Birmingham, originally developed by Tim Johns (Johns 1994). Since Johns's retirement in 2001, this valuable resource for language learning has continued to be available through the English for International Students Unit (EISU) at the University of Birmingham. The pages are updated occasionally with new items. The information on this site is a direct result of issues that have emerged from second language students writing in English. This resource provides teachers with the results of corpus searches about particular aspects of language.

The Kibbitzers always begin with an excerpt from an actual student text to contextualize the example. The format of the Kibbitzer then varies from providing concordance examples to exercises with answers available through a separate link to a discussion of how a feature should be used in a particular context. The amount of explanation depends on the language feature being explored.

For ease of use, the Kibbitzers are divided into the categories of vocabulary, grammar, discourse, academic areas, and first language. It is also possible to see all 81 Kibbitzers at once in list form. For example, at the vocabulary level, in Kibbitzer 8, the user is given examples of when to use the words *illustrate*, *account for*, and *explain*. An example of a grammatical Kibbitzer is the exploration of when to use *reason to* versus *reason for*.

Your turn

Log onto www.eisu.bham.ac.uk/support/online/kibbitzers.shtml. This will take you to the main page of the EISU Kibbitzer site. From the right-hand side of the page select "Lexis (Vocabulary)" then click on the word *pose*. Work through the Kibbitzer to see the different types of information and activities provided. List some of the different types of information used to help refine the use of this word.

The MICASE Kibbitzer uses the Michigan Corpus of Academic Spoken English (MICASE) as the resource for searches. MICASE has approximately 1.8 million words, with more than 190 hours of transcribed speech from various university settings including, for example, lectures, study groups, class presentations, and office hour meetings (Simpson et al. 2002). The MICASE project, as we will see later in this chapter, has a number of resources that can be extremely useful for teaching academic spoken English.

The MICASE Kibbitzer, available through the MICASE project Web site, was inspired by Tim Johns's Kibbitzers, but has some noteworthy differences. Because it is a much newer site, at this writing the MICASE

Kibbitzer has 14 topics as opposed to the 81 currently available on the University of Birmingham's site. In addition to the difference in number of topics available, there is also a significant difference in the format. The MICASE Kibbitzers are much more like mini research projects, or corpus-based language descriptions, using much more prose as opposed to the more skeletal approach of Johns's Kibbitzers. However, having more prose does not detract from the MICASE Kibbitzers. They are written in very accessible and reader-friendly language, but these Kibbitzers do require more work on the part of the teacher to transform the Kibbitzer information into a ready-to-use classroom activity.

Your turn

Log onto micase.elicorpora.info/micase-kibbitzers. This will take you to the Kibbitzer portion of the MICASE Web site. From the list of Kibbitzer topics, select *Announcements of Self-Repair*. Look through the information provided by the two authors of this Kibbitzer, Stephanie Marx and John Swales. Compare the type of information presented in this MICASE Kibbitzer with the information found in one of the Tim Johns's Kibbitzer entries. Can you think of some ways to use this information in your classes? Write down two ways you could use these sites.

These two Kibbitzer Web sites are a rich resource for creating lessons that target particular language structures that can be troubling to English learners. Below is a sample activity that can be used to help a teacher begin to use the Kibbitzers.

Sample Activity

1. Find two to five essays written by nonnative English-speakers. If you are not teaching, borrow some essays from a friend who is teaching.
2. Look through the essays and identify some words that students have misused or where better word choices could have been made.
3. Go to the two Kibbitzers presented to see if any information is available on the words that you have identified. If not, try to find an example of a Kibbitzer item in the essays.
4. Create a teaching activity using the information from a Kibbitzer to help students avoid this word choice problem in the future.

Now that we have explored some of the online resources that teachers can use for instruction, let's look at some ready-made, corpus-based resources that are available.

In addition to the material found in the Kibbitzer, the MICASE site offers teachers lessons that are based on corpus research. The lessons are freely available for teachers to download and use. The MICASE research team only asks that teachers who use the lessons let the lesson developer know that they are using the material and credit the developers for their work. At this writing, there are 12 different topics addressed in these ready-made lessons. The topics range from a lesson by Rita Simpson on the three commonly confused words *say*, *tell*, and *talk* to a lesson by India Plough on the more complex topic of listening for conversation patterns using MICASE sound files. These lessons can easily be accessed through the MICASE site.[3]

Your turn

Look through the list of topics presented in the Lesson Plan section of the MICASE Web site: lw.lsa.umich.edu/eli/micase/teaching.htm. Select two of the topics from the list of lesson plans. Carefully review these lessons. List the adaptations you would need to make in order to use these in your particular teaching context. Or, revise a lesson plan to suit your class needs so that it is ready to go. Remember to give credit to the author of the lesson plan.

An often overlooked resource for lesson plans is publisher Web sites. For example, the Cambridge University Press Web site for its corpus-based learner dictionaries[4] has links to lesson plans and student worksheets that help teachers better use the resources found in these dictionaries.

Resources for use with students

In addition to the teacher resources mentioned in the previous section, there is an increasing number of Web sites that have activities based on corpus research or resources that can be used with students with little to no modification. Review Chapter 2 for specific details about creating corpus-based activities for students.

One area of corpus research that has gained popularity over the past few years is the use of the Academic Word List (Coxhead 2000) as a source for principled academic vocabulary instruction. One of the most popular Web sites with activities related to the Academic Word List is Tom Cobb's Compleat Lexical Tutor.[5] Students and teachers have a number of corpus resources available to them from the main page of this site. For example, students can input texts that they have written and immediately see how

3. micase.elicorpora.info/esl-eap-teaching-materials
4. www.cambridge.org/elt/dictionaries/resources.asp
5. www.lextutor.ca/

the words that they use are distributed across the different frequency bands of the Academic Word List. In the Sample Activity below, you will use the Compleat Lexical Tutor site to compare the vocabulary used in two different types of texts.

Sample Activity

1. Choose two texts that represent different types of writing. Some ideas for possible texts include:
   an e-mail to a friend vs. an essay on an academic topic
   a paper from one of your students vs. a paper you wrote
   a letter to the editor from a newspaper vs. an article from the front page
2. Before you run the texts through the program, jot down some of the differences that you expect to find between the vocabulary used in the two texts.
3. Now you are ready to copy and paste the texts into the Vocabprofile link on the main page of the Compleat Lexical Tutor site. Process your texts and check your predictions.

Take time to explore some of the other features and tools you'll find on the Compleat Lexical Tutor site. There are many resources, such as vocabulary tests, a tool for creating vocabulary lists from texts, a tool for comparing two word lists, and a tool for highlighting the amount of vocabulary shared across two texts. This site is regularly updated, so check it every few months at least to see what's new.

Another useful resource is the Corpus Lab Web site.[6] This site has some links to ready-made activities and a number of tools that can be used to generate exercises. It is a free site, but you must register to use it.

In addition to the sites discussed in this section, there are others that have activities and resources for language learning, and new sites will no doubt regularly become available. Appendix B and the companion Web site for this book list additional sites with corpora and teaching resources.

Using online corpora

In this section the discussion will focus on three online corpora: the Corpus of Contemporary American English (COCA), the *Time* Magazine Corpus, and MICASE. These three corpora represent well-established and

---

6. www.corpuslab.com/

carefully developed corpora that exist on stable sites, and they therefore make a sound choice for use as a basis for the discussion of online resources. These sites are also useful resources for you and your students. The principles described in this section will cover a range of different types of analysis and will be transferable to other corpora and contexts. By the end of this section, you will cover the basic skills needed to independently conduct your own online corpus investigations and to guide your students in their use of online corpora.

The three corpora that are the focus of this chapter range from the specialized spoken academic texts of MICASE, to COCA, which captures the general uses of language across a range of spoken and written registers. The third corpus, the *Time* Corpus, is a somewhat specialized corpus consisting entirely of articles from *Time* magazine. Because the *Time* Corpus spans the years from 1923 to 2006, it can be used to investigate how language has changed over time, and it also provides a good example of the strong effect topic has on vocabulary. After a brief overview of these three corpora, each corpus will be used to investigate a language question through sample activities designed to present and practice the skills needed to use online corpora to create language teaching materials and activities.

An overview of MICASE

As mentioned earlier in this chapter, the MICASE corpus is a 1.8-million-word corpus of academic spoken language. The corpus covers many of the speech events that are typically encountered by students at American universities (e.g., class lectures, interactive classes, group discussions, office hour meetings). MICASE has been developed through the efforts of a team of researchers at the University of Michigan in Ann Arbor in coordination with their English Language Institute. The online interface is extremely user-friendly and allows the user to specify an impressive number of variables. The screen shot in Figure 3.1 shows the range of variables that can be specified.

Sound files are also associated with the online transcripts and can be accessed to enhance the pedagogical value of this corpus for classroom instruction. In addition to the Web interface, a copy of MICASE can be ordered for use on a home computer, thus allowing greater versatility based on your interests. Currently, a written corpus is being compiled, thus promising to provide a well-rounded resource for teachers and language researchers.

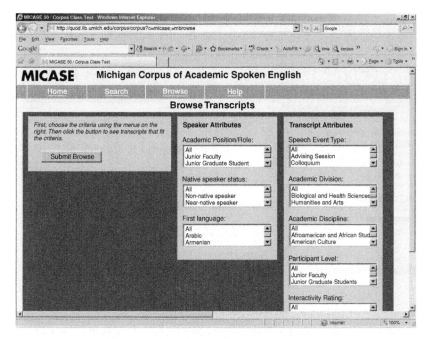

Figure 3.1: Screen shot of the variables in MICASE (Simpson et al. 2002).

The next two corpora, COCA and the *Time* Corpus, are a result of the efforts of Mark Davies at Brigham Young University.[7] The online format is the same for both of these corpora and is very user-friendly. Unlike MICASE, these corpora are only available online due to copyright restrictions.

An overview of the Corpus of Contemporary American English

COCA at this writing is a more than 400-million-word corpus of texts from 1990 through 2009. The goal is to update the corpus at least twice a year, adding another 20 million words each year. The registers in the corpus are newspaper, fiction, magazine, academic prose, and spoken language. All of the material comes from existing resources, and no texts were collected specifically for this corpus.

The COCA Web site allows the user to search by register and to compare features across registers. The corpus is also tagged for parts of speech

7. corpus.byu.edu/

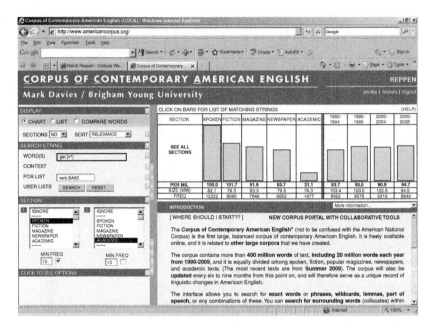

Figure 3.2: A screen shot with the results on a search of the verb *get* in COCA (Davies 2008–).

(POS), allowing users to perform specific grammatical searches. For example, a user can compare particular verbs in conversation with those found in academic prose. Or, a user can look to see which prepositions typically follow certain verbs in passive voice (e.g., *His answer was based on the reading*). The search function is designed to display results by register, and also by decade, allowing the user to see changes in the use of certain words or structures over time. Figure 3.2 shows a screen shot comparing the use of the verb *get* across the registers and over the decades. The display format shown in Figure 3.2 is the chart display; results can also be displayed as a list.

Looking at the right-hand side of the screen shot in Figure 3.2, we see that the use of *get* during the last four decades has not varied much. This lack of variation is clearly seen in the bar graph display. The normed counts (a computation method that allows for accurate comparisons of texts of different lengths) range from 83.7 to 94.7 times per million words, also reflecting the lack of variation across the decades. But, when we look at the use of the verb *get* across registers, and particularly at the two registers of academic prose and spoken language, we see a dramatic difference in the patterns of use. We see that *get* is very frequent in conversation

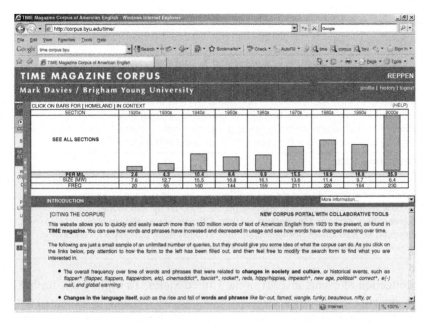

Figure 3.3: A screen shot with the results of a search on the word *homeland* in the *Time* Corpus (Davies 2007–).

(150.0 times per million) and not so frequent in academic prose (21.1 per million). The user could then click on the bar graph display for each register and see KWICs (Key Word In Context) of the target form *get* in those registers, which will be discussed in more detail in the next section.

An overview of the Time *Corpus*

The third, and final corpus, that we will use in this chapter is the *Time* Corpus. This corpus of 100 million words from *Time* magazine is divided by decade. This allows the user to see changes in the language over time, not only the addition of particular words that have entered the language, such as *blog* or *Internet*, but also to see how the use, or collocations, of certain words have changed over time. Some of these changes reflect technological advances, such as the introduction of new words like *blog*, while other changes reflect current events and "hot" topics. For example, in Figure 3.3 we see a screen shot from the *Time* Corpus for the results of a search on the target word *homeland*.

The bar graph on the upper right-hand side of Figure 3.3 clearly shows that in the last decade the use of the word *homeland* has increased greatly,

Table 3.1: *KWICS from the 1940s and 2000s for the target word* homeland

KWICS from 1940

has forgotten how insular the little **homeland** is. Last week, after six sudden
regular Army units to defend the **homeland** consisted of 1,250,000 home troops
and defense of the German **homeland**. Without the successful warding off of
who fled from their Nazi-controlled **homeland** last July in a 38-ft. pilot sloop
and that the "Jewish national **homeland**" promised by Great Britain in 1917
who fled to Germany when his **homeland** was restored to France.
In this confusion, with their **homeland** fully occupied and under Hitler's

KWICs from 2000

on technological improvements in **homeland** defense. Chat with him on Tuesday
and his staff at the Office of **Homeland** Security want to use the Sit Room
the new White House Office of **Homeland** Security run by Tom Ridge, with all
to give voters increased **homeland** security. Officials across the country
approved $8.3 billion for **homeland** security in December, but only $1.5 billion
Tommy Thompson and **Homeland** Security chief Tom Ridge often looked

a reflection of events in 2001 in the United States. To explore this further,
we can click on the bar graphs. For example, we can look at the use of the
word *homeland* for the decades 1940 and 2000, both times when the United
States was involved in conflicts, to see if the meaning, or use, of *homeland*
has shifted. Table 3.1 shows a random selection of KWICS for the target
form *homeland* from these two decades.

As we can see from the KWICs, in the 1940s the word *homeland* was
almost always a noun used to refer to a geographic space associated with
a particular group. In the examples from the 2000s *homeland* is almost
always used as an adjective to modify the noun *security*, or as a proper noun
to refer to a political office (the Office of Homeland Security).

These brief examples show some of the many ways that online corpora can
be used to explore aspects of language use and tease out particular aspects
of language. In the next section, we will look at three detailed examples of
how to use each of these online corpora in the language classroom.

Using online corpora for classroom activities and materials

In this section, after providing some general guidelines for using online
corpora for developing teaching materials and activities, each of the three
corpora discussed previously will be used to provide a detailed example of
developing a teaching resource. Across all of these examples there are some

basic principles that are used to structure the development of resources or activities. The guidelines presented serve as a reminder of the factors to consider when developing materials and activities with online corpora.

Some general guidelines for using online corpora

Although by no means comprehensive, this checklist is offered as a starting point to develop activities using online corpora.

Checklist for developing activities with online corpora
- Have a clear idea of the point that you want to teach.
- Select the corpus that is the best resource for your lesson.
- Explore the corpus completely for the point you want to teach.
- Make sure that your directions are complete and easy to follow.
- Make sure that your examples focus on the point that you are teaching.
- Provide a variety of ways for interacting with the materials.
- Use a variety of exercise types.
- If you are using computers, *always* have an alternative plan or activity in the event of computer glitches.

In the next three sections, a detailed example of a classroom activity will be presented in a step-by-step fashion to exemplify the range of different activities that can be explored through the three online corpora highlighted in this chapter. In addition to demonstrating the range of topics, these example activities highlight the different processes that can be used to explore these online corpus resources and create activities.

Using MICASE for teaching spoken language – an example activity

One area that is often problematic for language students is realizing the different spoken and written demands of language in an academic context. Most students know that the informal spoken language used with peers is not language that they should use to write academic papers. As students interact in classes, it is usually through spoken language, yet spoken language in the classroom also differs from the informal language of interacting with peers. The MICASE corpus has a wealth of spoken language information and can be used in a number of ways to inform instruction and create activities. In this example activity we are going to take a slightly different approach from the activities seen thus far in the book. Instead of looking at a frequency list, or picking a particular word or phrase and looking at its context of use in KWICs, we are going to look at an example of a word that has several meanings, the word *well*, and examine how this word is distributed across a range of different contexts.

From the MICASE site, in addition to generating KWICs with links to the transcripts and sound files, the user is able to view the results of a search as tables that show the distribution of the search term across a range of variables. So, after entering in our search term, *well*, in the same way that we would for a search generating KWICs, we can choose any of several ways to view the results. In the case of our search on the word *well*, we could choose to view the distribution by gender, academic discipline, level of lecture interactivity (i.e., highly interactive vs. low). For the purposes of this activity we are choosing to view the results of *well* by the context of use (see Table 3.2).

As you see, Table 3.2 shows the transcript file name, the speech event (or context of use), the total number of occurrences of *well* in that particular file (matches), the total number of words in that file (word count), and last but certainly not least in importance, the normed count (frequency/10,000 words). A normed count allows texts of unequal length to be compared. For example, the raw counts (matches) for the number of *well*s in the media union service encounter is 11. The raw count for the number of *well*s in the social psychology dissertation defense is 9, yet when we look at the normed counts, we see that the normed count for the dissertation defense is 7.32 vs. 5.76 for the service encounter. This is because the text of the service encounter is longer, so when the ratio is computed it takes text length into consideration, allowing us to accurately compare across texts of different lengths. For a more detailed description of norming see Methodology Box 6 in Biber, Conrad, and Reppen (1998).

So what can we do with this information? Well, one activity could be to see which texts have the highest normed counts for *well* and then go to those texts and see if *well* is being used as a filler (in the same way as *uh* or *um*), as a discourse marker (as at the beginning of this sentence), or as an adverb (as in *He did well on the test*). Seeing if there are any common characteristics across the texts with either high or low uses of *well* might also be insightful. However, just looking at the numbers without going back to the transcripts could create a distorted view of *well*. So a second or follow-up activity could be to have students look at the texts and categorize the uses of *well* that they find in the transcripts. This type of activity can be a very engaging learning experience as students sort out the different meanings and uses of a word, providing multiple exposures of the target form in context.

Table 3.2: *MICASE results for* well *by speech event*

Transcript ID	Speech Event Title	Matches	Word Count	Frequency/ 10,000 words
LAB205SU045	Hydraulics Problem Solving Lab	85	10398	81.74
COL999MG053	Career Planning and Placement Workshop	11	14842	7.41
DEF500SF016	Social Psychology Dissertation Defense	9	12280	7.32
SVC999MX104	Media Union Service Encounters	11	19072	5.76
STP175SU141	Teaching Biochemistry Student Presentations	10	18587	5.38
MTG999ST015	Forum for International Educators Meeting	8	17323	4.61
LEL565SU064	Principles in Sociology Lecture	5	12371	4.04
LES495JU063	Political Science Lecture	53	15359	34.5
LEL542SU096	Perspectives on the Holocaust Lecture	3	9258	3.24
LES330JG052	Graduate Industrial Operations Engineering Lecture	24	11098	21.62
SEM475JU084	First Year Philosophy Seminar	3	13906	2.15
ADV700JU023	Honors Advising	19	9519	19.96
OFC150MU042	Astronomy Peer Tutorial	31	21798	14.22
DEF420SF022	Music Dissertation Defense	21	15516	13.53
SEM140JG070	Graduate Buddhist Studies Seminar	28	26075	10.73
OFC195SU116	Heat and Mass Transfer Office Hours	22	20603	10.67
STP355MG011	Bilingualism Student Presentations	3	15956	1.88
DIS315JU101	History Review Discussion Section	3	16708	1.79
DEF270SF061	Artificial Intelligence Dissertation Defense	3	21594	1.38
ADV700JU047	Academic Advising	2	28160	0.71
SEM475MX041	Graduate Philosophy Seminar	1	22214	0.45

Your turn

Can you think of other activities that you could do with this table? What other language features would you be interested in seeing displayed in a table like this?

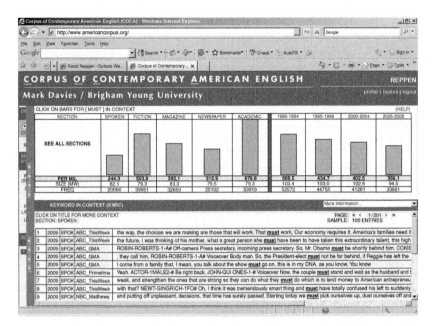

Figure 3.4: Register distribution and KWICs for *must* in COCA (Davies 2008–).

Using COCA to teach register awareness – an example activity

In this example activity we are going to use the COCA corpus. Since this corpus has five registers – spoken, fiction, magazine, newspaper, and academic – it is an ideal resource to see how language can vary across registers. For this activity we are going to use the word *must* and see how it varies in spoken and written texts. Once at the COCA site we enter in our search word, *must*, and select "chart" as the display format. The screen shot in Figure 3.4 shows the results of a search of *must* and how it is distributed across the five registers. As can be seen in Figure 3.4, *must* is most frequently found in academic texts and least frequently found in spoken language. These are the two registers that we will explore further by looking at the KWICs of *must*. To see the KWICs from the spoken and academic registers, we simply click on the bar graph for that register and the KWICs appear in the screen below the bar-graph display.

Table 3.3 (pages 48–49) shows 20 lines each for the spoken and academic registers from the KWICs for *must*. Looking at these two sets of KWICs, we can see that some differences emerge in the use of this word across the two registers. First, looking to the left of *must* we see in the spoken texts that personal pronouns (we, you, I) are frequently in subject position, however, in the academic texts inanimate nouns (the environment, the world, museums) or people referred to by their professions (teachers, kings) are often in the subject position.

Another difference between these two registers emerges as we read the KWICs. In conversation, *must* is not always used to convey obligation as it is in the academic texts. For example, in the following KWICs from the conversation register we see *must* used in a nonobligatory sense:

> For some, this **must** be déjà vu.
>
> Neil Entwistle **must** have, or in all likelihood, had information about how they were killed.
>
> I know this **must** be a terrible blow for them.
>
> I **must** have had something to hide so I'm guilty.

In the academic KWICs in Table 3.3 *must* is always used in the obligatory sense, except for the one time it is used as a noun. (Can you find that example?)

In Chapter 5 there is a step-by-step example of an activity using COCA to explore another aspect of spoken and written register differences that makes use of the part of speech resources available though this online corpus. In addition to the instructions available in Chapter 5 and Appendix A, the companion Web site has a PowerPoint presentation with instructions on how to use the COCA and *Time* corpora, with step-by-step screen shots.

Using the Time *Corpus for teaching academic writing – an example activity*

Since *Time* is a popular magazine written for a wide audience, it is a nice source of authentic, accessible, high-interest texts for low-intermediate to advanced language learners. In this third and final example, we will look at how to use the *Time* Corpus to examine verb choices in academic writing. We know from corpus linguistic research, and also from research on writing, that multiword verbs (phrasal or prepositional verbs) are not preferred in academic texts. For example, instead of writing *look into* in an academic paper, it would be a more appropriate choice to use one of the lexical verbs, *investigate* or *examine*. One writing activity that teachers often do with novice writers is to have students look at the verbs they are using and try to replace the multiword verbs with lexical verbs.

In this activity we will use the *Time* Corpus to compare the use of *look into* and *investigate*. To perform this search we will use the wildcard option. The wildcard option allows the use of certain characters (e.g., ? or *) to allow for other words or letters to be found so that the user does not have to

Table 3.3: *KWICs of* must *from spoken and academic registers*

Spoken KWICs of *must*

around California are on it, working 24-hour-long shifts. # For some, this **must** be déjà vu because they were out here just last month fighting the summit fire

It's far different from what the defendant is accused of doing. But judges **must** not only be neutral, they must appear to be neutral. And if he

defendant is accused of doing. But judges must not only be neutral, they **must** appear to be neutral. And if he has a proclivity or appears to have

He pursued a line of questioning which revealed that Neil Entwistle **must** have, or in all likelihood, had information about how they were killed,

his parents who are my generation and wonderful nice people, and I know this **must** be a terrible blow for them. : Finally though, Mr. Mayor,

Just yesterday Geraldine Ferraro, another New York political leader who you **must** know well – a former New York congresswoman. .: Oh yeah.

home schooling her three older children while meeting the twins special needs. Clothing **must** be customized. Diapers don't fit right. Feedings are difficult.

But just speaking for myself, what I find a little disingenuous, I **must** say, is to blame that on the fact that, for example, there

is the time for us to take control of our own energy future. We **must**. It's a matter of economic security, national security and environmental security as

of our own energy future by only relying on these new technologies. Although we **must** very much motivate investment in those new technologies, we also

Although we must very much motivate investment in those new technologies, we also **must** rely on nuclear, we must rely on clean coal, we must rely on

motivate investment in those new technologies, we also must rely on nuclear, we **must** rely on clean coal, we must rely on natural gas and, yes,

we also must rely on nuclear, we must rely on clean coal, we **must** rely on natural gas and, yes, we must rely on our own reserves

on clean coal, we must rely on natural gas and, yes, we **must** rely on our own reserves of oil as well. All right.

find out why in the world I was being accused of these things, I **must** have had something to hide so I'm guilty. # People who make false

American people expect us to get it done. In the work ahead, we **must** be guided by the philosophy that made our nation great. As Americans, we

collective wisdom of ordinary citizens. And so, in all we do, we **must** trust in the ability of free peoples to make wise decisions and empower them to

improve their lives for their futures. # To build a prosperous future, we **must** trust people with their own money and empower them to grow our economy. As

agreement that will keep our economy growing and our people working. And this Congress **must** pass it as soon as possible. # We have other work to do on

Our shared responsibilities extend beyond matters of taxes and spending. On housing we **must** trust Americans with the responsibility of home ownership and

Academic KWICs of *must*

may no longer be able to perform simple daily tasks with the same ease and **must** adopt new techniques to perform these activities. In addition, they need to coping and adjustment. However, the ongoing adaptation to living with a visual impairment **must** also be recognized. Gordon et al.'s (2002) discussion of with visual impairments as possible, professionals in rehabilitation services **must** be able to recognize who among those who are affected require more support This recommended protocol does require quite a bit of class time and means that teachers **must** grade tests as soon as possible after they are given. Possibly Continent is in Confusion. Before long I expect to hear that the three kings **must** settle the matter by dividing America between them. " (n23) It is that with Great Britain under the Royal Proclamation, then in the beginning it **must** have appeared to be even better. Just as the proclamation was a corollary to its desire to acquire title to the land for just that purpose. McGillivray **must** have been gratified to read in the document that " the Generous mind of his If neuroscientists are to prevent their work from being misrepresented in this way, they **must** think more critically about how their research is presented to their research is presented to educators and the public, and in particular they **must** be very cautious about even the most innocent speculation about the practical

leading the faculty, is no longer sufficient. The arena in which the CAO **must** now play includes a large set of players, all with demands of their own Land, 2003). " Now more than in the past, CAOs **must** consider and confront legislative and legal mandates, greater student demands for a consumer friendly scientific enterprise. Now, is dealing with the colonial past a **must** for all museums? I spent considerable time working on those issues in Tervuren and etc. Needless to say, ethnographic museums are neither a panacea for, nor **must** their role in society be defined by such issues. If attendance must be a nor must their role in society be defined by such issues. If attendance **must** be a concern, improving it must not compromise the independence and ethics of South-South commerce, which China and India are leading. African leaders **must** be proactive and take advantage of the opportunities created by China's and that serve Africa's self-interest. And the rest of the world **must** work to ensure that Africans can benefit from these new patterns of international commerce. to alleviate environmental barriers and make living easier, the environment **must** be assessed to prevent falls in the home that could result in injury or even and the lack of round-the-clock water service create hardships. Someone **must** be available to collect water whenever it appears at the community faucet or community faucet or whenever the water truck shows up. Someone **must** carry home multiple heavy pails of water from the community faucet or the village or the village well and store it in large barrels or tubs. Someone **must** do all the water-related household tasks by transferring water from the large barrels and

49

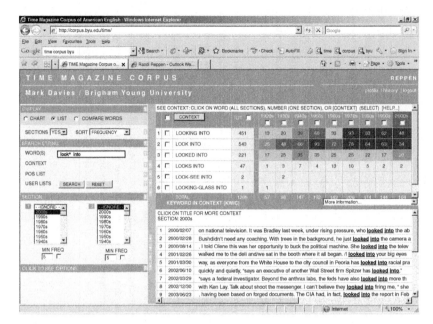

Figure 3.5: Screen shot of *look into* search using the wildcard " * " in the *Time* Corpus (Davies 2007–).

enter in each possible form of the word or phrase that they are searching. In this case we want to be able to find all the forms of *look into* (*looked into*, *looking into*, *looks into*) with all the forms of *investigate* (*investigated*, *investigates*, *investigating*) and compare the occurrence of these forms. So when we enter our search terms we will use the wildcard " * ", which in the *Time* Corpus allows any number of characters to occur in the position where the wildcard symbol is placed. One at a time, we will enter the following terms into the search field: *look* into*; *investigate**; *investigating*. This will allow us to find all the forms of *look into* and *investigate*. Figure 3.5 shows a screen shot with the display from *look* into*. The right-hand portion of the screen shows the "hits," and if we click on one of the boxes to the right of the term that we are interested in, the results, the KWIC, appears at the bottom of the screen.

Using the KWICs that appear for *look into*, or any of the other forms (e.g., *looked into*), you can have students see where it would be appropriate to use *investigate*. For example, in the five lines below that were copied and pasted from the KWICs of the *Time* Corpus, *investigate* could be substituted for *look into* in all of the examples except the first one.

Look into the glass, you will find the measure of one.
As investigators **look into** the causes of the crash

A panel of experts convened by the British government to **look into** cell-
phone use, found no direct indication that cell phones are harmful
You know these developments must be reaching critical mass when two
museums decide simultaneously to **look into** them.
Attorney General Janet Reno has agreed to **look into** it

Using student writing as a starting point for the multiword verbs being
used, and then having students use the corpus to find single-word or lexical
verbs that express the same meaning, can be a good vocabulary-building
exercise with a direct application to improving student writing. Simply
noting the difference in the frequency of use of *look into* and *investigate* in
the *Time* Corpus is an awareness-raising activity.

Putting it all together

In this chapter we have covered a lot of territory. We began with some general
guidelines for evaluating online resources and concluded with three specific
examples of activities with online corpora. The checklists and guidelines in
this chapter should be useful in your future explorations. The three detailed
examples using online corpora in different ways should provide you with a
solid background in the techniques used for creating activities with online
corpora. In the next chapter you will see how to create other activities and
also how to create corpora for use in your particular classes.

4 Using corpus material in the classroom and creating corpora for class use

In this chapter you will get answers to the following questions:

- How can I create corpus materials for my classes?
- How do I develop hands-on corpus activities?
- How can I create corpora for my classes?

Creating corpus materials for classroom use

As you have seen in the previous chapters, there are many ways to use corpora in the language classroom. As teachers, you are probably already quite familiar with creating materials for activities and lessons that address a variety of skills and topics. So, this section isn't intended to duplicate information you already have and that is covered more thoroughly in books that focus specifically on materials development, but will only address aspects that are particular to developing materials from corpora.

In Chapters 2 and 3 you have seen a variety of activities using corpora and corpus resources. These have also, in many cases, included creating materials for the activities. As with any materials creation, the focus of the material should be the teaching point. What are you trying to present or practice? Corpus materials are ideally suited for creating a range of different teaching materials. First, KWICs can be used to introduce a new structure or to raise awareness about a language pattern. For example, students could be presented with KWICs of singular and plural regular nouns and be asked to see if they can spot the change that takes place when a regular noun goes from singular to plural (add an -s or -es). At a more advanced level, students could be presented with KWICs and asked to look at subject / verb agreement issues or to discover the meaning of vocabulary words through the use of KWICs. A second way to use material from a corpus is to provide a rich context for practice. KWICs provide students with an opportunity to see a word or structure in high concentration, that is, multiple exposures in a short period of time. This is a powerful learning tool. Any of these KWIC activities can be created without too much effort on the part of the teacher. Copying and pasting KWICs from a corpus into a word-processing document is not difficult or time-consuming. By copying and pasting KWICs, teachers can modify or delete difficult or inappropriate vocabulary items.

Frequency lists are a useful beginning point for vocabulary instruction and can be used in a variety of ways, as seen in Chapter 1. A printed frequency list can be a springboard for several vocabulary activities. For example, students can scan for familiar and unfamiliar words or look for suffixes or prefixes. If there is access to computers, students can enter the unfamiliar words from a frequency list into the search function of one of the online corpora and see if they can determine the meaning of the unfamiliar word. Classes can be divided into teams to do vocabulary activities with the online KWICs. While at first this might seem a slow way to learn words, it can actually be more engaging than having students simply look up a word in the dictionary and write out the meaning or an example sentence or two. The KWIC activity has the added benefit of exposing the students to the words that frequently co-occur with the target vocabulary word, thus increasing learning.

Developing hands-on activities

Anytime students are actively involved in learning, student learning is enhanced and learning is more enjoyable. All of the activities that have been presented in this book have been hands-on activities. It is actually more difficult to create non-hands-on activities when using corpora or corpus resources.

There are two types of hands-on activities. One involves you as the teacher creating and bringing in printed material from a corpus or corpus research (like we saw in Chapter 2). The other involves having students use computers and search through corpora. The activities presented in this book have all been done by students, so you already have a rich resource of hands-on activities! For developing hands-on activities for students, here are a few guidelines to help make everything go smoothly:

- Be very familiar with the activity and work through each step *before* doing the activity with your students.
- Have very clear step-by-step directions.
- If you will be using a new Web site, walk students through the process as a model.

- Ask students to have only the current Web site open and walk around to help any students who are having difficulty.
- If you are using computers, always have a backup plan in case something goes wrong.

Your turn

Think of your students or the students you expect to teach. Are there any other tips that you would add to the list? Write down any new ideas.

Creating corpora for classroom use

What do I do first?

Each year, the number of corpora that are available for use is increasing. So, before tackling the task of building your own corpus, make sure that there is not an existing corpus that meets your needs. That said, as a teacher, you are probably interested in exploring types of language that are usually not represented by existing corpora, such as a corpus of your students' papers, or a corpus of class readings. In this case you will need to build a corpus.

Your turn

What kind of texts will you be using in your classes? Are your students studying a specialized use of language (e.g., business, nursing, landscaping). List some of the corpus resources that you would like to use with your students (e.g., a corpus of biology research articles, a corpus of business memos) or use your list from Chapter 1. Look in Appendix B to see if anything on your list is mentioned in the information on the resources listed there. If not, try searching on the Web. If you still don't see what you are looking for, you will want to carefully read this section about creating a corpus for your class.

The best way to guide your corpus building is to have a goal or question to focus your collection. Having a clear goal is an essential first step in corpus construction, since this will guide the design of the corpus. In language classes, most times you will be creating relatively small corpora for class use and not creating large corpora that represent all aspects of language use. So your first step is to think about the type of language that you want to collect and have a clear goal in mind. Do I want a corpus of my students' writing? Do I want to create a corpus from the readings we are doing?

What kind of data do I use and how much?

The question of corpus size is a difficult one. Remember from Chapter 1 that there is not a specific answer to this question. Corpus size is certainly not a case of one size fits all. For our purposes as language teachers, small but representative is more important than millions of words. In our case, the question of size will be resolved by two factors: representativeness (Have I collected enough texts [words] to accurately represent the type of language I am interested in?) and practicality (time constraints). In some cases it is possible to completely represent the language being studied. For example, it is possible to capture all the papers written by your students for a particular assignment, or to make a corpus of the readings that students will be working with, or texts from a particular event (e.g., letters to the editor related to a class topic, political speeches in the last local election). In these cases, complete representation of the language can be achieved. In some cases, however, it is not possible to achieve complete representation, and in these cases corpus size is determined by capturing enough of the language for accurate representation. For example, if you are interested in teaching students how to use reporting verbs (e.g., *report*, *discuss*, *claim*) in academic articles, you certainly will not collect every academic article that has been written. A corpus of 30 to 40 academic journal articles will probably contain enough examples of reporting verbs to adequately meet your needs for this task.

How do I collect texts?

Now that you have a clear goal to guide your collection, you can begin to build your corpus. The next task is identifying the texts and developing a plan for text collection. In all cases, before collecting texts it is important to have permission to collect them. When collecting texts from people or institutions, it is essential to get consent from the parties involved. The rules that apply vary by country, institution, and setting, so be sure to check before beginning collection.

There are texts that are considered public domain. These texts are available for personal use or research, and permission is not needed. Public domain texts are also available for free, as opposed to copyrighted material, for which in addition to obtaining permission prior to use, you may also have to pay a fee. Even when using texts for private research, it is important to respect copyright laws. This includes material that is available online.

When creating a corpus there are certain procedures that are followed regardless of whether the corpus is representing spoken or written language. Some issues that are best addressed prior to corpus construction include:

What constitutes a text?
How will the files be named?
What information will be included in each file?
How will the texts be stored (what file format)?

WHAT CONSTITUTES A TEXT?

In many cases what constitutes a text is predetermined, but in some cases it is not. If you are collecting a corpus of your students' in-class writing, a text could be defined as all the essays written in the class on that particular day, or a text could be each student's essay. The latter is the best option. It is always best to create a text file at the smallest "unit," since it is easier to combine files than it is to have to open a file, split it into two texts, and then resave the files with new names. So, even if you are creating a corpus of in-class writing with the goal of comparing across different classes, having the essays stored as individual files rather than as a whole class will be best.

HOW WILL THE FILES BE NAMED?

Deciding how you are going to name files needs to be established before saving a text. Creating file names that include aspects of the texts that are relevant will be helpful. For example, if you are building a corpus of "Letters to the Editor" from newspapers that represent two different demographic areas (e.g., urban vs. rural) and are interested in the gender of the letter writer, then it would be useful to include this information in the file name. In this case, abbreviating the newspaper name, including the writer's gender, and also including the date of publication, would create a file name that is reasonably transparent and also a reasonable length. For example, a letter written by a woman in a city in Arizona printed in October of 2009 could have a file name of: azcf109. It is ideal if file names are about seven characters. If additional space is needed, after the first seven characters a dot (.) followed by three additional characters can be used. File names of this length will not cause problems with corpus tools or software backup tools.

WHAT INFORMATION WILL BE INCLUDED IN EACH FILE?

In many cases a *header* is included at the beginning of each corpus file. A header contains information about the file. This might include demographic information about the writer or speaker, or it could include contextual information about the text, such as when and where it was collected and under what conditions. If a header is used, it is important that the format of the header is consistent across all files in the corpus. Since creating a corpus is a huge time investment, it is a good idea to include any information in the header that might be relevant in the future. Headers often have some type of formatting that helps to set them apart from the text. The information might be placed inside angle brackets (< >) or have a marking to indicate the end of the header and the beginning of the text. Here is an example of a header from a conversation file:

<File name = spknnov06.mf>
<Setting = two friends chatting at a coffee shop>
<Speaker 1 = Male 22 years old>
<Speaker 2 = Female 33 years old>
<Taped = November 2006>
<Transcribed = Mary Jones December 2006>
<Notes: Occasional background traffic noise makes parts unintel-
   ligible>

HOW WILL THE TEXTS BE STORED; THAT IS, WHAT IS THE FILE FORMAT?

Determining the file format for storing texts may seem inconsequential; however, saving files in a format that is not compatible with the tools that will be used will result in many extra hours of work. Most corpus tools work with the file format *plain text*. When scanning written texts, downloading texts from the Internet, or entering texts (keyboarding), you are always given an option as to how to save the file. From the drop-down menu with the Save As option on your word processor, chose the option *plain text* (or *ASCII*). If the text is already in electronic format and has been saved by a word-processing program, just open the file and use the Save As option as described above and select *plain text.*

Some other important decisions in corpus creation

Whether creating a corpus of spoken or written texts, there are decisions that are best made during the design phase. Creating a corpus of written texts is an easier task than building a corpus of spoken texts, but both have challenges associated with them. Often written texts are already in electronic format. However, if the texts you are collecting are not in electronic format, the texts will need to be entered in electronic form. If the texts represent learner language, novice writing, or children's writing, it is important to preserve the nonstandard spelling and grammar structures. These may be of keen interest. In this case, you will most likely create two versions of the corpus: an original version and one that has the spelling standardized – what I call a "clean" version. Decisions about how to treat any art or nonorthographic markings (e.g., arrows, lines) will also need to be made. These challenges pale in comparison to the many decisions that need to be made when collecting a spoken corpus.

First of all, a spoken corpus obviously does not exist in written form but will need to be recorded and then transcribed in order to be useful. Spoken texts can be collected with either analog or digital recorders. The sound quality and ease of storage of the digital sound files outweigh using analog recordings except in a very few cases of large-scale corpus collecting. Once the recordings have been made, it is necessary to transcribe them into an electronic format. Unfortunately, current speech-recognition software is not able to convert the spoken files into text files accurately enough for corpus-building purposes. Instead, creating text files from recorded speech is accomplished by individuals listening to the recordings and transcribing, or keying them, into the computer.

For digital recorders there are several freeware programs that can be used for listening to the digital speech recordings while transcribing the sound files. Voice Walker and Cool Edit are two popular programs. These programs have settings that allow the rate of speech to be slowed without distorting the sound quality, thus helping the person transcribing.

Before beginning to transcribe, there are several decisions that must be made. Some of the more common questions that need to be addressed prior to transcription include: How will reduced forms (*gonna* instead of *going to*) be transcribed? As mentioned in Chapter 1, if the speaker says *wanna* or *gonna* for *want to* or *going to*, will what the speaker actually said be transcribed, or will the complete form be transcribed? Many times it is difficult to hear or understand what was said; this can be due to background noises or the speaker not being near the recording device. What will be transcribed in these instances? The transcriber can make a best guess and indicate that by typing a question mark in parentheses – (?) – after the guessed word. Or, the transcriber might simply write *unclear* and the number of syllables (e.g., *unclear – two syllables*) after the utterance.

Overlapping speech is another challenge in transcribing natural speech events. Speakers often talk at the same time or complete each other's turns. Deciding how this will be transcribed is helpful. Will the overlap be color coded as in the MICASE corpus? Will a bracket (e.g., { or [ ) be used to show the overlap? Often listeners will use conversational facilitators or minimal responses (*uh huh, mmm, hum,* etc.) to show that they are listening and attentive to what the speaker is saying. These overlaps and insertions are a challenge for transcribers. It is a good idea to standardize the spelling of these conversational facilitators. For example *mmm* might always be spelled with three *m*s, or the reduced form of *because* might always be spelled as *cuz*. How laughter will be transcribed is another decision that needs to be made. Making these decisions ahead of time will save many hours of anguish as you search files for particular features, only to realize that you need to spend time standardizing these forms.

Repetitions (*I – I – I want to eat pizza.*) and pauses are also features of spoken language that require transcribing decisions. Will pauses be timed? Or will the transcriber simply note short (maybe two to five seconds in length) and long pauses (maybe those longer than six seconds) through the use of dots, maybe three (. . .) for short pauses and six (. . . . . .) for long pauses? Again this decision will be informed by the goals for the corpus. Some corpora are carefully transcribed and include prosodic information (tone changes or rising and falling intonation; see Cheng, Greaves, and Warren 2008). This type of transcription is very time-consuming, but it allows researchers to capture many of the aspects of spoken language that are typically lost through the transcription process. This type of transcription is beyond the goals of most classroom corpora.

In most cases teachers will be creating written corpora, and after reading the details of the process involved in creating a spoken corpus, those who were thinking about collecting one may well change their minds.

Creating a corpus for class use can also be a project that involves students. They can be involved in keying in texts or reading scanned texts to make certain that the texts were scanned correctly (a great real-world proofreading activity).

Creating a corpus of class readings can be a rich resource for a variety of class activities, and having a corpus of writing from your students can be a tremendous time-saver for the teacher. These two resources can be a springboard for a wide range of tasks, and with corpus tools, can easily be used to create instructional materials.

Putting it all together

Thus far, you have been exposed to information that has provided a general introduction to corpus linguistics, outlined principles for developing materials and using corpora in the classroom, and seen specific examples of creating activities. At this point, you are able to use information from corpus-based research to inform teaching decisions, use online corpus resources and corpora that are available to you as a teacher, and to develop materials and activities from corpora and corpus resources.

In the next chapter, you will see examples of actual classroom activities that put all the aspects presented in this book all together and into practice. Hopefully you will have ideas of activities that you want to try.

5 Bringing it into the classroom: Example activities and descriptions of corpora in the classroom

In this chapter you will get answers to the following questions:

- What are some examples of activities that I can use in my classroom?
- How have other teachers used corpora with their students?

The format of this chapter is quite different from the preceding ones. This chapter provides five detailed examples of activities that can be used in classes and five examples of how language classes have used corpus activities and materials with students. The examples presented in this chapter range from introducing vocabulary to students as a prereading activity to developing register awareness through examining texts. Most of the examples presented in this chapter could take place in a wide range of language classrooms and levels. Hopefully you will see direct applications to the classes you are teaching or that you will be teaching. For these examples it is assumed that you have read the previous chapters and are acquainted with terms and processes used in interacting with corpora, such as loading texts, creating KWICs, and making frequency lists.

Example activities

This section presents five examples of classroom activities that have been used successfully in language classes. The activities cover a range of student proficiency levels from beginner to advanced. At the beginning of each activity the student level and the focus of the activity is stated. As you read through these activities, think about how you might use them in your classes. You may need to alter the activities to suit your teaching goals, but these five examples should provide you with a good starting point for using corpora in your language classroom.

Activity 1: Vocabulary activity for prereading

Level: Beginner
Activity focus: Reading and vocabulary

Step 1:   Ask students to load two to three newspaper texts and create a word frequency list (see Appendix A for details of how to do this using MonoConc Pro), or use the list provided in Appendix A.

Step 2:   Have students scan the frequency list and write down any unfamiliar or unknown words and the frequency of those words, stopping after finding five unfamiliar or unknown words.

Note: If the words being identified occur very frequently, (e.g., they are among the top 20 most frequent words for that text), the students will probably have difficulty reading the text. If unknown words do not occur very frequently or only occur once, the students should be fine reading the text. This is a useful prereading activity to quickly determine the vocabulary difficulty of a text.

Extension activity: If there are only a few words that the students do not know, have students try to learn the word's meaning by entering the word in the concordancer and using KWIC to discover the meaning from the context.

Activity 2: Register awareness through vocabulary

Level: Low-intermediate to advanced
Activity focus: Awareness of language use in different situations

Step 1:   Divide the class into two groups. Have students in one half of the class load 10 academic texts in a concordancer and the students in the other half of the class load 10 conversation texts. It does not matter if students select different texts from within the registers of academic texts and conversation as long as all 10 texts come from the same register. For example Student A may select texts 1 through 10 of the academic texts, while Student B might select academic texts 2, 4, 6, etc., through 20. Students may even use different corpora, as long as the register is consistent. (*Note*: If you do not have a corpus with academic and spoken texts, you can use COCA instead. See the Note below.)

Step 2:   Ask the students to create a frequency list from their texts that is arranged in frequency, not alphabetical, order. That is, the most frequent words are at the top of the list.

Step 3: Ask each student to write down the first 10 content words (nouns, verbs, adjectives, and adverbs), not function words (e.g., *the, an, a,* or prepositions).

Step 4: Ask students to compare their top 10 content words with a classmate who loaded the same register (i.e., comparing conversation with conversation or academic texts with academic texts) and consider the following questions: What are the top 10 content words the classmate found? Are any words the same?

Step 5: Now ask students to compare with a classmate who loaded the other register (i.e., comparing conversation with academic texts). Are any words the same? Discuss what differences students find within the same register and across the two registers.

Step 6: Ask students to think about their conversations with friends and about textbooks they read. How are conversations among friends similar to or different from the language in academic books?

Note: This should provide a springboard for a discussion about register and the need to consider the context of both spoken and written language.

If you do not have a corpus available with academic and spoken texts, COCA is a good resource for this activity. Have half the students use the academic register and half use the spoken register. The COCA site cannot create frequency lists, so use the extension activity.

Extension activity: Have students select a content word, then using a KWIC, see how that word is used in the texts. Does the word have the same use or meaning each time it is used? What do you learn from the KWIC that you cannot see by just looking at the frequency list?

Activity 3: Looking at discourse level with a focus on register awareness

Level: Intermediate to advanced
Activity focus: Spoken language in different contexts

Step 1: As a class, create a list of some of the different speaking situations that students are familiar with (e.g., friends chatting, phone conversations with family, a business meeting, class discussions, a formal speech).

Step 2: Make a list of situations on the board.

Step 3:   Now ask students to think about features of these situations (e.g., the speakers are strangers, the speakers are in the same place when interacting).

Step 4:   After discussing the situations that involve spoken language, make a chart and write down some of the situations and characteristics of these situations (see the chart example).

Note: Have students make their own charts. This can be done in pairs or on the board as a whole-class activity. The first two columns of the chart can be Situation and Situation Features. These columns should be completed at this point. Here is an example of a simple chart for recording situation, situation features, and text features:

Situation	Situation features	Text features
Friends talking	Interactive – two or more people talking	
	Friends share knowledge of each other	
Formal speech	One person speaking to many people	

Step 5:   Now, students should select texts from the corpus that reflect these different speaking situations (e.g., phone conversations, speeches, meetings). Students can work in pairs or individually. If the teacher prefers, students can be divided into teams, with each team working with a different register, or students can work individually and look across several situations.

Step 6:   After the students have described several situations, use a frequency list to compare some of the features found in these texts and fill in the Text Features column, as in the following example:

Situation	Situation features	Text features
Friends talking	Interactive – two or more people talking	Many pronouns: especially *I* and *you*.
	Friends share knowledge of each other	Lots of contractions
Formal speech	One person speaking to many people	Few contractions, many nouns

Step 7: After the students have completed their charts, discuss how the situational features (e.g., on the phone vs. face-to-face; with friends vs. with strangers) are reflected in the grammar and vocabulary of the various speaking situations. Have classmates or teams compare their findings.

Activity 4: Changing topics and asking for clarification

Level: Intermediate to advanced
Activity focus: Conversation

Step 1: Ask students to reflect on conversations with friends or classmates and to make a list of phrases or expressions that they use when they want to change the topic, return to an earlier topic, or ask for clarification. If students are having difficulty getting started, brainstorm some phrases and expressions as a class.

Step 2: Discuss how these phrases or chunks of language can be used in different situations.

Step 3: Now ask the students to load the conversation files from a corpus, or use the COCA site for this activity.

Step 4: Using a concordance program, have students search for the phrases that they wrote down. Ask the students to mark any of the phrases from their list that they find in the corpus.

Step 5: Have students look at Table 5.1, either on a handout or on an overhead transparency (OHT). This table contains a list of lexical bundles, or chunks of language, that were identified as part of a much larger analysis of language (see Biber et al. 1999 for more details). Are any of the phrases that the students came up with found in Table 5.1? Add any phrases that students listed and found in the corpus that are not in the table.

Table 5.1: *Lexical bundles from the* Longman Grammar of Spoken and Written English *(Biber et al. 1999)*

Lexical bundle	Purpose
Going back to...	Returning to an earlier topic
I would have thought...	Polite expression of disagreement
What we can do...	Proposing joint effort
The question is...	Explicit statement of issue
You mean to say...	Asks for confirmation of point speaker finds difficult to believe

Step 6: Now have students look for any of the expressions that are in Table 5.1 that students did not search for. Discuss some of the different situations when these expressions are used.

Activity 5: Looking at spoken and written language

Level: Low-intermediate to advanced
Activity focus: Writing and speaking – this activity will highlight the need to use language that is appropriate for the situation.

Note: This activity uses the COCA Web site. Instructions for using this site are included in the exercises in Appendix A and on the companion Web site for this book. Review Chapter 3 if more information is needed on using COCA.

Step 1: Ask students to discuss how they would ask a friend to loan them some money. Write some of the ideas and actual phrases on the board. Now ask the students how they would ask a family member for money. Again, write some of the ideas and actual phrases on the board.

Step 2: Look at some of the differences in the actual language used by the students and the different reasons as to why money should be loaned in these two situations. Use these differences to help raise awareness of how we use language differently depending on whom we are speaking or writing to (i.e., audience awareness).

Step 3: Ask students to go to the Web address: www.americancorpus.org. This site will be used to compare the use of *got to* across conversation and academic texts.

Step 4: On the left-hand side of the Web page under the heading DIS-PLAY, select CHART

Step 5: Under the heading SEARCH STRING, in the box next to WORD(S) enter: *got to*

Step 6: Under the heading SECTIONS, in 1, select SPOKEN

Step 7: Under the heading SECTIONS, in 2, select ACADEMIC
(Note: Steps 4 through 7 are the basic steps to carry out any type of search on this Web site. Of course, you can vary registers and target forms for searches.)

Step 8:   Now hit the Search button under SEARCH STRING.

Step 9:   Look at the upper right-hand side of the screen to see the chart of your search results. Use this information to answer the following questions:

Which register has the highest use of *got to*?
How does the use of *got to* differ in spoken texts and academic writing?

Extension activity: To see how *got to* is used in context, click on the bar in the chart for a register (e.g., spoken, academic). The KWIC for *got to* in that register will appear in the lower right-hand portion of the screen. Compare how *got to* is used in conversation and academic writing by looking at the KWICs.

Your turn

Think about the activities that you just read. Which ones would work in the classes that you teach? Select one activity presented in the previous section and describe how you would adapt it to fit your particular teaching context.

Examples from the classroom

The five examples described in this section provide snapshots of activities that teachers have used to incorporate corpora or information from corpus research into the classroom to enhance language learning. As you will notice from the examples, there is nothing earthshaking or highly unusual about the types of activities. As discussed in previous chapters, the activity types are often the same or similar to the types of activities that teachers regularly use in language classes. What is different is the content and how that content was determined. Using the information from a corpus or corpus activities, teachers can make certain that the structures that are being taught are the ones that students will encounter as they interact in English or that students are reading texts that are level appropriate.

Prereading activity

When selecting reading material, teachers often take a best guess as to the vocabulary load, or number of new words, that students will encounter. In an integrated-skills class that uses different themes throughout the semester, finding reading material that is at an appropriate level for the students can be a challenge. To help address this challenge, the teacher created a mini corpus of class reading materials from both online sources and textbook readings.

The textbook readings were scanned into the computer. Students then used a concordance program to create word lists in frequency order from the class readings. As in Activity 1 in the first section of this chapter, students marked unfamiliar words. The teacher then had an accurate assessment of the vocabulary load of the readings. If the students knew 85 to 90 percent of the words from the readings, the teacher knew that the students had the vocabulary knowledge to get the information presented in the readings, and the class could proceed with the readings. If the students encountered many unknown words, the teacher then created vocabulary-learning activities that were specifically targeted at the words that students needed to know in order to read the material. The activities included traditional, in-class, vocabulary activities and also activities that used KWICs from the readings. This prereading activity took the guesswork out of what to teach and also immediately informed the teacher as to the level appropriateness of the readings that were being used in the class. For other ways that this class reading corpus was used, read Donley and Reppen (2001).

Academic vocabulary development

Research has shown the importance of controlling vocabulary for success in academic classes, particularly the control of academic vocabulary (Schmitt & McCarthy 1997; Schmitt 2000). Variations of the example described in this section have been used in both academic-reading classes and integrated-skills classes. In order to help students become more aware of academic vocabulary, teachers have used information from the Academic Word List to identify the academic words in the texts that they are using.

Once the words have been identified, teachers have used several different approaches to raising awareness of these academic words. Some teachers have provided students with lists of the academic vocabulary words in the texts and had students look through the text to identify and highlight the target words. Other teachers have the texts in electronic format and typographically enhanced the words from the Academic Word List, using bold, underlining, or a different color font in order to help students notice the words. Typographic enhancement of academic vocabulary by the teacher or highlighting by students serves the same purpose as the typographic enhancement publishers use to raise awareness and make content-specific words or words being glossed more noticeable. Teachers with texts in electronic format have also had student teams create KWICs with sets of academic word lists and then create vocabulary activities. By using KWICs, students see the target word in context in a concentrated format since each line contains the target form. This type of activity can also be useful for raising awareness of frequent collocates for the target form.

An example from an advanced writing course

This section describes the use of KWICs as a resource for an advanced writing activity to increase the variety of verbs students use to incorporate information from outside sources when writing academic papers. When teaching writing to advanced ESL/EFL students or to novice first language writers, teachers need to help students learn how to include information from outside sources in their writing.

Academic writing regularly incorporates ideas and information from different sources. As students learn to write papers for their academic classes, they also need to be able to incorporate ideas and information from a variety of sources. Students need to be able to acknowledge the sources that they are using. Often students rely on the same set of verbs (e.g., *said*, *reported*) to indicate that they are incorporating information from an outside source. For example, "Smith (1997) said that..." In order to teach students to use a greater variety of verbs for citing outside sources, one teacher prepared a small corpus from online academic journals. Since academic journals regularly refer to outside sources, particularly in the introduction and literature-review sections, the journals provided a rich source of verbs used to incorporate information from sources.

First, as a resource to help students become aware of the variety of verbs available, the teacher provided students with KWICs of the verbs frequently used for citing sources (e.g., *report*, *present*, *describe*, *explain*). Next, the teacher used the Conceal Hits function of the MonoConc Pro KWIC program and created a handout for students to supply the verbs that could complete the sentences.

After completing these two activities, the teacher incorporated the information into the peer-editing process by having students circle the reporting verbs used when students were citing outside sources or incorporating information from outside sources. Each student had a copy of the KWICs listing a variety of verbs, so they were able to use this resource when writing and editing their academic papers. The teacher reported that the students enjoyed the activity and that several students were using the KWIC function to check their papers for other classes.

A conversation class

Although many ESL/EFL classes focus on academic language, students who are studying in an English-speaking environment also need to be able to interact in nonacademic situations. This activity describes how information from a corpus can be used to help language learners be more successful in service encounters. Using examples from a corpus of service encounters, a teacher developed some role-playing activities about ordering food and beverages at a coffee shop. The teacher wanted students to become aware of the linguistic resources that native speakers use in order to have additional time to think before making choices under the time constraints of ordering a food or beverage. Working in pairs, the students marked the fillers (e.g., *uh*, *um*) that they found in a transcript from a service encounter. The following are two excerpts with fillers in text samples from the T2K-SWAL corpus:

CUSTOMER: Hi. Could I get small regular coffee, with **uh**, hazelnut?
STAFF: Here's a large cup, because we ran out of the small ones.

STAFF: Hi.
CUSTOMER: I want just the onion bagel, and could I, **um**, have cream cheese? And a small lemon-lime.

After marking the fillers in the transcript, the students looked for any patterns. Just as in the two excerpts above, when customers needed to make a decision but were not certain of their final choice, they "bought time" through the use of a filler like *uh* or *um*. After this discussion, students used the transcripts as a role-play dialogue. The use of fillers is often not taught in ESL/EFL classes, yet it is an important feature of language use in certain contexts.

A beginning conversation class

This example does not use a corpus, but it does use information from corpus research to inform teaching choices. In a beginning ESL listening and speaking class, the teacher wanted to make certain that his students were as prepared as possible to face the real world of conversation that took place in their daily lives once they left the classroom. Using information from the *Longman Grammar of Spoken and Written English* (Biber et al. 1999), he knew that the 12 most frequent verbs used in conversation would give his students a foundation for understanding the conversations around them. Early in the course he began to introduce these 12 lexical verbs, even though they were irregular and often taught much later in non-corpus-informed syllabi. The 12 most frequent lexical verbs are: *say, get, go, know, think, see, make, come, take, want, give,* and *mean* (Biber et al. 1999, 373).

The teacher also knew that as the students gained proficiency, they would realize the many meanings of these verbs, but at least his students had a head start in mastering these verbs so frequently encountered in conversation.

Putting it all together

At this point you have learned how to use a variety of corpus tools. You have also read about various uses of corpora in the classroom. It is now time for you to think about, and act on, how to use this information in the classes that you are teaching now or will be teaching in the future. Hopefully you have enough information and ideas to launch forward successfully into the world of corpora in the classroom! Now it really is: Your turn!

Appendix A
Resources for activities and instructions for using COCA and MonoConc Pro

This appendix contains the following resources:

1. Prepared resources for use with activities, including:
   photocopiable word list in frequency order from a corpus of conversation
   photocopiable KWIC lines from a corpus of conversation
   photocopiable KWIC lines from a newspaper corpus
2. Three activities using COCA to explore language
3. An introduction to using MonoConc Pro

1. Prepared resources for use with activities

The 25 most frequent words from a conversation corpus of one million words

Frequency	Word
39457	the
39114	I
38147	and
30822	you
27106	to
23372	a
22864	that
20997	it
18067	of
13169	like
12916	in
12785	yeah
12653	so
12641	was
12526	is
11666	we
10951	know
10892	have
8977	just
8803	they
8617	it's
8543	what
8509	but
8490	this
8440	do

KWICs of well *from a conversation corpus of one million words*

That is basil but it's not doing very **well**.

Oh **well** never mind.

Oh **well** that's good.

Okay **well** we'll come home it's past our curfew

That's right you did not feel **well**. . . .

I said **well** we'll get up there again.

I'm sure, **well** you'll see her on graduation.

You might as **well** use them up.

She just doesn't style your hair very **well**.

She couldn't stop laughing and I go **well** that's some friend

Obviously he doesn't know you as **well** as I do.

I thought **well** that's real good

You can tell it's not working very **well**.

We might as **well** take the table over to Mary tonight.

Well what a terrible way to end a book.

KWICs of well *from a newspaper corpus of twenty-five thousand words*

He planned to be in the running as **well**.

The Lakers' could find themselves waiting **well** into the summer for the right deals.

Whelan said, his choice to appear, as **well** as the work of his private charitable foundation on behalf . . .

That connection doesn't sell **well** in California – and Dan Lungren proved it.

Prospective cosmetic-surgery patients need to think carefully about the risks as **well** as the benefits before submitting to any purely elective procedure.

It can occur spontaneously in some people, too, for reasons not **well** understood.

Some of the guys on this team who deserve to go as **well**.

Some have access to income-tax revenues at their sites as **well**.

And you're going to play **well** and you're still going to lose.

When we play **well**, things are going our way.

His psyche had been ripped apart, as **well**.

2. Three activities using COCA to explore language

The Corpus of Contemporary American English (COCA) is free to use, but you are asked to register. By registering you will have access to expanded functions, such as making notes on searches. Registering will not include you in any mailing lists.

Go to www.americancorpus.org and click on ENTER to access the corpus and use it for these activities.

Activity 1. Exploring got to *in spoken and academic language*

On the left-hand side of the screen, enter the following:

1. At DISPLAY, select CHART
2. At SEARCH STRING, WORD(S), enter *got to*
3. At SECTIONS, 1, select SPOKEN
4. At SECTIONS, 2, select ACADEMIC
5. At SEARCH STRING, click on SEARCH
   Look at the upper right-hand side of the screen to see your search results. Which register has the highest use of *got to*?
   (*Note:* These are the five basic steps for any search you carry out. Of course, you can vary registers and target forms.)
6. To see the target word(s) (*got to*) in context, on the right-hand side of the screen, click on the bar in the chart for the register (e.g., spoken, academic) you want to see KWICs for. You will see the KWIC in the lower right-hand portion of the screen.

You can highlight your results (either the table or the KWIC) and copy and paste them to a word processor using regular Windows commands.

Activity 2. Explore using a word and a part-of-speech (POS) tag

Explore the differences between the copular (verb + adjective) form and the noncopular form. To do this comparison you will need to run two separate searches, one for the copular form and one for the noncopular form.

Follow the same steps as in Activity 1, but in step 2 do the following:

At SEARCH STRING, WORD(S), enter *turn*
Click on POS LIST, from the drop-down menu select *adj.ALL*

After doing this search go back and

Click on POS LIST, from the drop-down menu select *noun.ALL*

What register differences do you see?
Do you notice anything about the words that go with the copular form of *turn*?

Activity 3. Exploring make and take: Two commonly confused words in L2 classes

Search for *make* + noun then search for *take* + noun. Use the same steps as in Activity 2 and select *verb.ALL* or *noun.ALL* from the POS LIST to do these searches.

This activity can be useful to help students become aware of the collocates of these two often misused verbs.

3. An introduction to using MonoConc Pro

This introduction assumes that you own a copy of MonoConc Pro or have access to a computer lab that has MonoConc Pro installed.

Remember: The texts you use in MonoConc need to be in "plain text" format. If you are using texts that were created or saved in Word, simply use the *save as* function from the *File* drop-down menu choices. In the box labeled "Save as type" just underneath the place for the file name, select *plain text* as the option for the way to save the file. If you are copying texts from the Web, save them as plain texts using the *save as* function.

Getting started

1. Click on the MonoConc icon located on your desktop.
   You should see a light gray screen with two pull-down menu options: *File* and *Information*.
   (*Note:* It might be useful to resize the screen to full size by selecting the full screen option from the upper-right corner.)
2. Select the *File* pull-down menu.
   Then select *load corpus files* – **not** *load corpus url* (unless you are loading texts from a Web site).
   (*Note:* You can select *count words and tokens while loading*.)

3. Go to the C prompt (c:) (either by using the pull-down menu or clicking on the folder with the "up" arrow on it, to the right of the pull-down box) and select the corpus that you want to work with.

You can select texts by highlighting them with your cursor: Multiple texts can be selected by using CTRL + left click (on the mouse button). If you want to select a block of texts from a directory, select the first text and then move the cursor to the last text and SHIFT + left click – all the texts should be highlighted. To select an entire directory use CTRL + A.

Wait while the texts load – this does not take long (you will see a progress bar to show that the computer is working on your request). When the corpus is loaded, the number of files (and the number of words and tokens if you selected that option) will appear in the lower bar of the MonoConc window. The directory that you are working in is also displayed. In the newer version a Type/Token ratio also appears in the lower bar display.

4. Close the window that shows the texts.

Now you should see four (4) pull-down menu options:

File; *Concordance*; *Frequency*; *Information*

5. Select the pull-down menu *Frequency* and then select the option: *Corpus frequency data* – This generates a frequency list in alpha or frequency order.

After looking at the frequency list, close the window.

Generating concordance lines (KWICs)

1. Select the *Concordance* pull-down menu, and then select *search*.
2. Enter the term(s) that you want to explore. Enter only one search term at a time. (That is, do not enter *commit, committed* – the program will look for those two terms to co-occur!) You can search phrases or expressions, just not several terms at the same time (unless you use the Boolean search function).
3. The display screen is split. If you click on a KWIC line, that line and its context will appear in the upper portion of the window. The windows can be resized by placing the cursor on the "bar" that divides the windows. When the cursor changes from an arrow to a small bar with arrows pointing up and down, the window can be resized by left clicking and moving the cursor to resize the window.

The number of hits is displayed in the lower-left corner of the MonoConc screen. These numbers can be used to make cross-register or corpus comparisons.

Note: If you are working with a tagged corpus and do not want to use tags, do the following after generating each concordance.

Go to the *Display* (or *Corpus text*) pull-down menu: select *suppress*, select *tags*, then

Go to *Display* (or *Corpus text*) again and select *context type*; in *context options*, use the pull-down menu to select *words*. The default is then 8 (you can change this if you want more context, but since you can always get more context in the upper window of the display, 8 is a good choice).

Note: The following wildcards are quite useful in generating concordances.

* = 0 or more characters
(e.g., *paint** = *paint, paints, painted, painting, painter*, etc.)
% = 0 or 1 character
(e.g., *paint%* = *paint, paints*; colo%r = *color, colour*)
? = exactly 1 character
(e.g., *thr?w* = *throw, threw*)

4. Sorting concordance lines: This can be a useful way to identify patterns. Collocations can be sorted to the right or left of the search term. Sorting one way and then the other often reveals different patterns and can provide useful data. It is also possible to do multiple sorts (e.g., first to the right of the search term and then two words to the right of the term).

Note: Once a concordance is generated, some new pull-down menus will appear in the upper bar: *Display; Corpus text; Sort; Window*.

To sort concordance lines select the *Sort* pull-down menu. Then select the type of sort that you want (e.g., search term = first term right; first right / first left; etc.).

To see which collocates have the strongest association with the target word, select the *Frequency* pull-down menu – then select *collocate frequency data*. This will generate a display with the strongest associations for the target term. This can be useful in identifying trends (e.g., verbs that co-occur with the target word; word classes that have strong associations, etc.). MonoConc highlights words that have strong associations, but this collocate frequency table format sometimes makes the information more accessible to the researcher.

You can save an output in two ways: 1). Go to the *Concordance* pull-down menu and select *save as* – remember to give the file a "transparent" and descriptive name. 2). Go to the *Display* pull-down menu and select *Copy to the clipboard.*

Note: You can delete any unwanted hits by highlighting the hit(s) and using CTRL + D. The number of hits is automatically updated when this is done.

Settings

You can change the settings to make your corpus searches easier. There are three kinds of setting changes that might be useful.

Note: Remember to check these settings if you are using a computer that is also used by someone else.

1. Number of hits displayed – If you are looking at an item that is *very* frequent, you might want to constrain the number of hits displayed. MonoConc will take a random sample from the total hits and show the number you select. For example if the feature that you selected resulted in 1,000 hits, and you wanted to see only 500, MonoConc would only display 500 randomly selected hits from the 1,000 that were found.

   To set or check the Number of hits displayed: Go to the pull-down *Concordance* menu and select *Search options*. At the top of the *Search Options* window you see *Max. search hits*. Change this to reflect the *maximum* number of hits that should be displayed.

   Note: If you want all hits to be displayed, set the number to be very large (e.g., 100,000).

2. Minimum number – If you are interested in seeing only features that occur with some regularity you can change the minimum number of hits needed for an item to be displayed. Perhaps you want only items that occur at least 10 times. Then you would change the setting of minimum number to 10. This will be reflected in the frequency list that is generated and also in the concordance lines that you are looking at.

   To set or check the Minimum number: Go to the pull-down *Frequency* menu and select *Frequency options*. Near the middle of the *Frequency options* window you see a pull-down menu labeled *Minimum frequency*. Change this to reflect the *minimum* number of hits.

3. Amount of context – you can change how much context you see in the concordance display (or use instructions given above).

To set or check the <u>Amount of context,</u> go to the pull-down *Concordance* menu and select *Search options*. In the middle of the *Search options* window you see two pull-down menus: *Context type*; *Size*. Change this to increase or decrease the amount of context displayed with each concordance line. Remember that you also can click on a concordance line and get the display in the upper window of the *Concordance* screen.

Note: If you are comparing features across registers or corpora, be sure to load one corpus or subcorpus to do your searches, and then unload the corpus/subcorpus/registers before rerunning your searches on the next corpus/subcorpus/registers. You will need to record findings to be able to compare across corpora or registers.

Appendix B
Corpus resources and tools

Links to corpora and corpus information

American National Corpus (ANC)
www.americannationalcorpus.org
An under-construction corpus based on the same design as the BNC, but with American English and material from 1990 on. The site has samples of the corpus format and links to papers related to the ANC project.

British National Corpus (BNC)
www.natcorp.ox.ac.uk
A 100-million-word, multiregister corpus of spoken and written British English, searchable by word or phrase. In addition to information about the BNC, the site has links to many resources. *Note:* Accessing the BNC through Mark Davies's site, corpus.byu.edu, allows a few more search options.

Corpus.BYU.edu
corpus.byu.edu
This site links to the many corpora that are searchable through Mark Davies's interface. The format for searches is the same regardless of the corpus. The interface is user-friendly and also allows for part-of-speech and wildcard searches. This site has one of the best interfaces with the BNC for word and phrase searches that include graphs and tables of search results by register.

Corpus of Contemporary American English (COCA)
www.americancorpus.org
An online, searchable 400+-million-word corpus of American English arranged by register, including news, spoken, and academic texts. The texts in this corpus are from 1990 to the present. This site allows the user to also search by part of speech (POS).

Corpus of Spoken Professional American English (CSPAE)
www.athel.com/cspa.html
A 2-million-word corpus of professional spoken language (meetings, academic discussions, and White House press conferences). A 42,722-word sample is available for free.

ICAME – International Computer Archive of Modern and Medieval English

icame.uib.no

A site with links to information and corpus resources.

ICE – International Corpus of English

www.ucl.ac.uk/english-usage/ice/index.htm

The site has information about the availability of several spoken and written 1-million-word corpora of various world Englishes. The corpora follow the same format and provide a rich resource for cross comparisons.

Lampeter Corpus of Early Modern English Tracts

khnt.hit.uib.no/icame/manuals/LAMPETER/LAMPHOME.HTM

About 1 million words of material from English pamphlets printed between 1640 and 1740. The pamphlets cover a range of subjects from religion to economics.

MICASE – Michigan Corpus of Academic Spoken English

micase.elicorpora.info

This free, online, searchable corpus of academic spoken language is a valuable resource. The online concordancer is user-friendly and has a number of search options. The corpus is also available for purchase for a modest fee. This site has links to lesson materials that have been prepared based on MICASE. There is also a free shareware program for transcription that can be downloaded.

Scottish Corpus of Texts and Speech

www.scottishcorpus.ac.uk/corpus/search

A Scottish corpus of spoken and written texts and a search tool.

SUSANNE Corpus

www.grsampson.net/Resources.html

This is a 130,000-word subset of the Brown corpus that has been annotated with the SUSANNE scheme. SUSANNE tries to represent several aspects of English grammar that can be useful for natural language processing (NLP) research. This page also has links to the CHRISTINE and LUCY corpora.

Time Magazine Corpus

corpus.byu.edu/time

This online corpus of *Time* magazine from 1923 through 2006 is searchable through Mark Davies's user-friendly interface (see Corpus.BYU.edu on page 83). The *Time* Corpus allows interesting explorations of how language changes over a relatively short period of time.

Links to corpus tools

AntConc
www.antlab.sci.waseda.ac.jp/software.html
This freeware program can create word frequency lists and KWICs. This easy-to-use program also identifies n-grams of 2 to 6 words.

AWL Highlighter
www.nottingham.ac.uk/~alzsh3/acvocab/awlhighlighter.htm
This site allows the user to input texts and highlights the words from the Academic Word List (AWL). It also has links to exercises, a gap-making program for fill-in-the-blank exercises, and other useful sites.

Business Letter Concordancer (BLC)
someya-net.com/concordancer/index.html
This site links users to a concordancer that accesses several corpora, including a corpus of business letters, personal letters, and letters of historic figures (e.g., Thomas Jefferson, Robert Louis Stevenson).

Collins Cobuild Corpus Concordance Sampler
www.collins.co.uk/Corpus/CorpusSearch.aspx
This site allows the user to search a 56-million-word corpus. Forty concordance lines are provided for each search.

Collocate
www.athelstan.com
This reasonably priced program identifies collocates and generates n-grams (aka word clusters) and provides some statistics (e.g, mutual information, t scores).

Compleat Lexical Tutor
www.lextutor.ca
In addition to access to various corpora and tools, this site allows you to input texts for vocabulary analysis. The site also has many useful articles on corpora and language teaching, and tests for assessing vocabulary are also available.

Conc (from Summer Institute of Linguistics)
www.sil.org/computing/conc
A freeware concordancing program that runs on a Mac.

Concordancing
www.nsknet.or.jp/~peterr-s/concordancing/index.html
A site with links to information about using concordancing and information about concordancing programs. It also has a bibliography of concordancing

books and articles (the most recent is 1998, though, so it might be out-dated).

Kfngram
www.kwicfinder.com/kfNgram/kfNgramHelp.html
A site that has online concordance and collocation resources. This site allows users to input and search corpora.

MonoConc
www.athelstan.com/mono.html
This affordable and easy-to-use concordancing package provides concordances, frequency lists, and collocate information.

Multiconcord
artsweb.bham.ac.uk/pKing/multiconc/l_text.htm
A description of development and use of this multilingual parallel concordancer available for purchase or to acquire a demo version.

Paul Nation's Web page
www.victoria.ac.nz/lals/staff/paul-nation/nation.aspx
This page has many links to information about vocabulary. It also has a download of a free program, Range, to compare target texts with two wordlists (the General Service List and the Academic Word List).

SCP – Simple Concordance Program
www.textworld.com/scp
This free program works for both Windows and Macintosh. It also works with different languages.

Ultrafind
www.ultradesign.com/ultrafind/ultrafind.html
A freeware program for Macintosh that can do text searches.

WebCONC
www.niederlandistik.fu-berlin.de/cgi-bin/web-conc.cgi?sprache=
    en&art=google
This online software does KWICs with many languages.

Web Concordancer
www.edict.com.hk/concordance
A free concordancing program and links to several corpora including Brown and Lancaster Oslo Bergen (LOB). This site also allows users to input and search a corpus.

WebCorp
www.webcorp.org.uk
A concordancer that uses Web search engines with the World Wide Web as a corpus.

WordSmith
www.lexically.net/wordsmith
A concordancing program that, in addition to creating concordance lines, provides other information (e.g., frequency, key words, mutual information scores, word length, etc.). A powerful tool for searching a corpus.

Miscellaneous Links

Cool Edit
www.adobe.com/special/products/audition/syntrillium.html
A freeware program for transcription.

Hot Potatoes
web.uvic.ca/hrd/halfbaked
A Web site with software that can be used to design activities. This software allows the user to create a number of different activities from matching to fill-in-the-blank to timed reading. This is a useful resource for teachers wanting to create corpus-based activities.

T2KSWAL – TOEFL 2000 Spoken and Written Academic Language
TOEFL Monograph #25
www.ets.org/portal/site/ets/menuitem.c988ba0e5dd572bada20bc47
c3921509/?vgnextoid=73d7457727df4010VgnVCM10000022f95190
RCRD&vgnextchannel=d35ed898c84f4010VgnVCM10000022f95190
RCRD
TOEFL Monograph #25 can be accessed from this site. This monograph reports on research carried out on a corpus of 2 million words of spoken and academic language from four universities across the United States. (See *TESOL Quarterly* 36, 9–48 for full description.) The corpus is not available to the general public.

University of Lancaster
Center for Computer Corpus Research on Language
ucrel.lancs.ac.uk
This is a rich resource for corpus and corpus linguistics information.

Selected bibliography of corpus linguistics and language teaching

Aarts, J. 1991. Intuition-based and observation-based grammars. In K. Aijmer and B. Altenberg, eds., *English corpus linguistics*. London: Longman.

Altenberg, B., and Granger, S. 2001. The grammatical and lexical patterning of MAKE in native and non-native student writing. *Applied Linguistics* 22 (2), 173–94.

Aston, G. 1995. Corpora in language pedagogy: Matching theory and practice. In G. Cook and B. Seidlhofer eds., *Principles and practice in applied linguistics*, pp. 257–70. Oxford: Oxford University Press.

———. 1997. Enriching the learning environment: Corpora in ELT. In A. Wichmann, S. Fligelstone, T. McEnery, and G. Knowles, eds., *Teaching and language corpora*, pp. 51–64. London: Longman.

———. 2000. Corpora and language teaching. In L. Burnard and T. McEnery, eds., *Rethinking language pedagogy from a corpus perspective*, pp. 7–17. Frankfurt: Peter Lang.

———. 2001a. Learning with corpora: An overview. In Aston, G.. ed., *Learning with corpora*, pp. 4–45. Houston, TX: Athelstan.

———. ed. 2001b. *Learning with corpora*. Houston, TX: Athelstan.

Barbieri, F., and Eckhardt, S. 2007. Applying corpus-based findings to form focused instruction: The case of reported speech. *Language Teaching Research* 11 (3), 319–46.

Biber, D. 1993. Representativeness in corpus design. *Literary and Linguistic Computing,* 243–57.

———. 2006. *University language*. Amsterdam: John Benjamins.

Biber, D., Conrad, S., and Leech, G. 2002. *Longman student grammar of spoken and written English*. London: Longman.

Biber, D., Conrad, S., and Reppen, R. 1998. *Corpus linguistics: Investigating language structure and use*. Cambridge: Cambridge University Press.

Biber, D., Conrad, S., Reppen, R., Byrd, P., and Helt, M. 2002. Speaking and writing in the university: A multi-dimensional comparison. *TESOL Quarterly* 36, 9–48.

Biber, D., Johansson, S., Leech, G., Conrad, S., and Finegan, E. 1999. *Longman grammar of spoken and written English*. Harlow, Essex: Pearson Education.

Biber, D., and Reppen, R. 2002. What does frequency have to do with grammar teaching? *Studies in Second Language Acquisition* 24, 199–208.

Botley, S. P., McEnery, A. M., and Wilson, A. eds. 2000. *Multilingual corpora in teaching and research*. Amsterdam: Rodopi.

Bowker, L., and Pearson, J. 2002. *Working with specialized corpora: A practical guide to using corpora*. London: Routledge.

Braun, S. 2005. From pedagogically relevant corpora to authentic language learning contents. *ReCall* 17 (1), 47–64.

Brodine, R. 2001. Integrating corpus work into an academic reading course. In G. Aston. ed., *Learning with corpora*, pp. 138–76. Houston: Athelstan.

Burnard, L., and McEnery, T. eds. 2000. *Rethinking language pedagogy from a corpus perspective: Papers from the Third International Conference on Teaching and Language Corpora*. Frankfurt: Peter Lang.

Carter, R. 1998a. Orders of reality: CANCODE, communication, and culture. *ELT Journal* 52, 43–56.

Carter, R., and McCarthy, M. 1995. Grammar and the spoken language. *Applied Linguistics* 16, 141–58.

———. 1997. *Exploring spoken English*. Cambridge: Cambridge University Press.

———. 2004. Talking creating: Interactional language, creativity and context. *Applied Linguistics* 25 (1), 62–88.

———. 2006. *Cambridge grammar of English: A comprehensive guide to spoken and written English grammar and usage*. Cambridge: Cambridge University Press.

Carter, R., Hughes, R., and McCarthy, M. 2000. *Exploring grammar in context*. Cambridge: Cambridge University Press.

Chan, T., and Liou, H. 2005. Effects of Web-based concordancing instruction on EFL students' learning of verb-noun collocations. *Computer Assisted Language Learning* 18 (3), 232–50.

Cheng, W., and Warren, M. 2000. The Hong Kong Corpus of Spoken English: Language learning through language description. In L. Burnard and T. McEnery, eds., *Rethinking language pedagogy from a corpus perspective*, pp. 133–44. Frankfurt: Peter Lang.

Cobb, T. 1997. Is there any measurable learning from hands-on concordancing? *System* 25, 301–15.

———. 1999. Breadth and depth of lexical acquisition with hands-on concordancing. *Computer Assisted Language Learning* 12, 345–60.

Collins COBUILD English Grammar. 1990. London: Collins.

Collins, H. 2000. Materials design and language corpora: A report in the context of distance education. In L. Burnard and T. McEnery, eds., *Rethinking language pedagogy from a corpus perspective*, pp. 51–63. Frankfurt: Peter Lang.

Conrad, S. 1996. Investigating academic texts with corpus-based techniques: An example from biology. *Linguistics and Education* 8, 299–326.

———. 1999. The importance of corpus-based research for language teachers. *System* 27, 1–18.

———. 2000. Will corpus linguistics revolutionize grammar teaching in the 21st century? *TESOL Quarterly* 34, 548–60.

———. 2001. Variation among disciplinary texts: A comparison of textbooks and journal articles in biology and history. In S. Conrad and D. Biber. eds.,

Variation in English: Multi-dimensional studies, pp. 94–107. Harlow, Essex: Longman.

———. 2002. Corpus linguistic approaches for discourse analysis. *Annual Review of Applied Linguistics* 22, 75–95.

Conrad, S., and Biber, D. 2009. *Real grammar: A corpus-based approach to English.* Harlow, Essex: Pearson/Longman.

Cook, G. 1997. Language play, language learning. *ELT Journal* 51, 224–31.

Cortes, V. 2004. Lexical bundles in published and student disciplinary writing: Examples from history and biology. *English for Specific Purposes* 23, 397–423.

Csomay, E. 2005. Linguistic variation within university classroom talk: A corpus-based perspective. *Linguistics and Education* 15, 243–74.

Coxhead, A. 2000. A new academic word list. *TESOL Quarterly* 34, 213–38.

Dahlmann, I., and Adolphs, S. 2009. Multi-modal spoken corpus analysis and language description: The case of multi-word expressions. In P. Baker, ed., *Contemporary approaches to corpus linguistics*, pp. 125–39. London: Continuum Press.

De Cock, S. 1998. A recurrent word combination approach to the study of formulae in the speech of native and non-native speakers of English. *International Journal of Corpus Linguistics* 3 (1), 59–80.

Donley, K. M., and Reppen, R. 2001. Using corpus tools to highlight academic vocabulary in SCLT. *TESOL Journal* 10, 7–12.

Ellis, N. C., Simpson-Vlach, R., and Maynard, C. 2008. Formulaic language in native and second-language speakers: Psycholinguistics, corpus linguistics and TESOL. *TESOL Quarterly* 42, 375–96.

Flowerdew, J. 2001. Concordancing as a tool in course design. In M. Ghadessy, H. Mohsen, A. Henry, and R. Roseberry, eds., *Small corpus studies and ELT: Theory and practice*, pp. 71–92. Amsterdam: John Benjamins.

Flowerdew, L. 1998. Integrating 'expert' and 'interlanguage' computer corpora findings on causality: Discoveries for teachers and students. *English for Specific Purposes* 17, 329–45.

———. 2005. An integration of corpus-based and genre-based approaches to text analysis in EAP/ESP: Countering criticisms against corpus-based methodologies. *English for Specific Purposes* 24, 321–32.

Friginal, E. 2006. Developing technical writing skills in forestry using corpus-informed instruction and tools. Paper presented at the American Association of Applied Corpus Linguistics Conference, Flagstaff, Arizona.

Gaskell, D., and Cobb, T. 2004. Can learners use concordance feedback for writing errors? *System* 32 (3), 301–19.

Gavioli, L. 1997. Exploring texts through the concordancer: Guiding the learner. In A. Wichmann, S. Fligelstone, T. McEnery, and G. Knowles. eds., *Teaching and language corpora*, pp. 83–99. London: Longman.

———. 2001. The learner as researcher: Introducing corpus concordancing in the classroom. In G. Aston, ed., *Learning with corpora*, pp. 108–137. Houston, TX: Athelstan.

———. 2005. *Exploring corpora for ESP learning.* Philadelphia: John Benjamins.

Gavioli, L., and Aston, G. 2001. Enriching reality: Language corpora in language pedagogy. *ELT Journal* 55, 238–46.

Gledhill, C. 2000. The discourse function of collocation in research article introductions. *English for Specific Purposes* 19, 115–35.

Gilquin, G., Granger, S., and Paquot, M. 2007. Learner corpora: The missing link in EAP pedagogy. *Journal of English for Academic Purposes* 6, 319–35.

Gómez-González, M. A. 1998. A corpus-based analysis of extended multiple themes in PresE. *International Journal of Corpus Linguistics* 3, 81–113.

Granger, S. ed. 1998. *Learner English on computer.* London: Longman.

———. 2003. The International Corpus of Learner English: A new resource for foreign language learning and teaching and second language acquisition research. *TESOL Quarterly* 37, 538–46.

Granger, S., Hung, J., and Petch-Tyson, S. eds. 2002. *Computer learner corpora, second language acquisition and foreign language teaching.* Amsterdam: John Benjamins.

Granger, S., and Tyson, S. 1996. Connector usage in the English essay writing of native and non-native EFL speakers of English. *World Englishes* 15, 17–27.

Henry, A., and Roseberry, R. 2001. Using a small corpus to obtain data for teaching a genre. In M. Ghadessy, H. Mohsen, A. Henry, and R. Roseberry, eds., *Small corpus studies and ELT: Theory and practice*, pp. 93–133. Amsterdam: John Benjamins.

Hewings, M., and Hewings, A. 2002. "It is interesting to note that . . . ": A comparative study of anticipatory 'it' in student and published writing. *English for Specific Purposes* 21, 367–83.

Hickey, R. 2003. *Corpus presenter.* Amsterdam: John Benjamins.

Hinkel, E. 2003. Simplicity without elegance: Features of sentences in L1 and L2 academic texts. *TESOL Quarterly* 37, 275–301.

Horst, M., Cobb, T., and Nicolae, I. 2005. Expanding academic vocabulary with an interactive on-line database. *Language Learning and Technology* 9 (2), 90–110.

Holmes, J. 1988. Doubt and certainty in ESL textbooks. *Applied Linguistics* 9, 21–43.

Hughes, R., and McCarthy, M. 1998. From sentence to discourse: Discourse grammar and English language teaching. *TESOL Quarterly* 32, 263–87.

Hunston, S. 2002a. *Corpora in applied linguistics.* Cambridge: Cambridge University Press.

———. 2002b. Pattern grammar, language teaching and linguistic variation: Applications of a corpus-driven grammar. In R. Reppen, S. Fitzmaurice, and D. Biber, eds., *Using corpora to explore linguistic variation*, pp. 167–83. Amsterdam: John Benjamins.

Hunston, S., and Francis, G. 1998. Verbs observed: A corpus-driven pedagogic grammar of English. *Applied Linguistics* 19, 45–72.

———. 2000. *Pattern grammar: A corpus-driven approach to the lexical grammar of English.* Amsterdam: John Benjamins.

Hunston, S., Francis, G., and Manning, E. 1997. Grammar and vocabulary: Showing the connections. *ELT Journal* 51, 208–16.

Hyland, K., and Milton, J. 1997. Qualification and certainty in L1 and L2 students' writing. *Journal of Second Language Writing* 6, 183–205.

Johns, T. 1994. From printout to handout: Grammar and vocabulary teaching in the context of data-driven learning. In T. Odlin, ed., *Perspectives on pedagogical grammar*, pp. 293–313. Cambridge: Cambridge University Press.

———. 1997. Contexts: The background, development and trailing of a concordance-based CALL program. In A. Wichmann, S. Fligelstone, T. McEnery, and G. Knowles, eds., *Teaching and language corpora*, pp. 100–115. London: Longman.

Jones, R. 1997. Creating and using a corpus of spoken German. In A. Wichmann, S. Fligelstone, T. McEnery, and G. Knowles, eds., *Teaching and language corpora*, pp. 146–56. London: Longman.

Kennedy, G. 1987. Quantification and the use of English: A case study of one aspect of the learner's task. *Applied Linguistics* 8, 264–86.

———. 1998. *An introduction to corpus linguistics*. London: Longman.

Kilgarriff, A. 2001. Comparing corpora. *International Journal of Corpus Linguistics* 6, 1–37.

Knight, D., and Adolphs, S. 2008. Multi-modal corpus pragmatics: The case of active listenership. In J. Romeo, ed., *Corpus and pragmatics*, pp. 175–90. Berlin: Mouton de Gruyter.

Kurzet, R. 2002. Teachable moments: Videos of adult ESOL classrooms. *Focus on Basics*, 5(D), 8–11.

Lawson, A. 2001. Rethinking French grammar for pedagogy: The contribution of spoken corpora. In R. Simpson and J. Swales, eds., *Corpus linguistics in North America*, pp. 179–94. Ann Arbor: University of Michigan Press.

Lee, D., and Swales, J. M. 2006. A corpus-based EAP course for NNS doctoral students: Moving from available specialized corpora to self-compiled corpora. *English for Specific Purposes* 25, 56–75.

Leech, G. 1997. Teaching and language corpora: A convergence. In A. Wichmann, S. Fligelstone, T. McEnery, and G. Knowles, eds., *Teaching and language corpora*, pp. 1–23. London: Longman.

———. 1999. The distribution and function of vocatives in American and British English. In H. Hasselgård and S. Oksefjell eds., *Out of corpora*, pp. 107–18. Amsterdam: Rodopi.

Lewandowska-Tomaszczyk, B. ed. 2003. *PALC2001: Practical a pplications in language corpora*. Frankfurt: Lang.

———. ed. 2004. *PALC2003: Practical applications in language corpora*. Frankfurt: Lang.

Lindemann, S., and Mauranen, A. 2001. "It's just real messy": The occurrence and function of '*just*' in a corpus of academic speech. *English for Specific Purposes* 20, 459–75.

Mauranen, A. 2003. The corpus of English as lingua franca in academic settings. *TESOL Quarterly* 37, 513–27.

McCarthy, M. 1998. *Spoken language and applied linguistics*. Cambridge: Cambridge University Press.

McCarthy, M., and Carter, R. 1995. Spoken grammar: What is it and how can we teach it? *ELT Journal* 49, 207–18.

———. 2001. Size isn't everything: Spoken English, corpus, and the classroom. *TESOL Quarterly* 35, 337–40.

———. 2004. There's millions of them: Hyperbole in everyday conversation. *Journal of Pragmatics* 36, 149–84.

McCarthy, M., McCarten, J., and Sandiford, H. 2004/2006. *Touchstone Levels 1–4*. New York: Cambridge University Press.

McCarthy, M., and O'Dell, F. 1997. *Vocabulary in use*, upper intermediate. Cambridge: Cambridge University Press.

———. 2001. *Basic vocabulary in use*. Cambridge: Cambridge University Press.

———. 2004. *English phrasal verbs in use*. Cambridge: Cambridge University Press.

———. 2005. *English collocations in use*. Cambridge: Cambridge University Press.

McEnery, T., and Wilson, A. 1993. The role of corpora in computer-assisted language learning. *Computer Assisted Language Learning* 6 (3), 233–48.

———. 1996. *Corpus linguistics*. Edinburgh: Edinburgh University Press.

———. 1997. Teaching and language corpora. *ReCall* 9 (1), 5–14.

McEnery, T., Wilson, A., and Baker, P. 1997. Teaching grammar again after twenty years: Corpus-based help for teaching grammar. *ReCall* 9 (2), 8–16.

McKenna, B. 1997. How engineers write: An empirical study of engineering report writing. *Applied Linguistics* 18 (2), 189–211.

Meunier, F. 2002. The pedagogical value of native and learner corpora in EFL grammar teaching. In S. Granger, J. Hung, and S. Petch-Tyson, eds., *Computer learner corpora, second language acquisition and foreign language teaching*, pp. 121–41. Amsterdam: John Benjamins.

Meunier F., and Granger, S. eds. 2008. *Phraseology in foreign language learning and teaching*. Amsterdam and Philadelphia: John Benjamins.

Meyer, C. 2002. *English corpus linguistics*. Cambridge: Cambridge University Press.

Milton, J. 1998. Exploiting L1 and interlanguage corpora in the design of an electronic language learning and production environment. In S. Granger, ed., *Learner English on computer*, pp. 186–98 London: Longman.

Mindt, D. 1996. English corpus linguistics and the foreign language-teaching syllabus. In J. Thomas and M. Short, eds., *Using corpora for language research: Studies in the honour of Geoffrey Leech*, pp. 232–47. London: Longman.

Mudraya, O. 2006. Engineering English: A lexical frequency instructional model. *English for Specific Purposes* 25, 235–56.

Mukherjee, J., and Rohrbach, J. M. 2006. Rethinking applied corpus linguistics from a language-pedagogical perspective: New departures in learner corpus research. In B. Kettemann and G. Marko, eds., *Planning, gluing and painting corpora: Inside the applied corpus linguist's workshop*, pp. 205–232. Frankfurt: Peter Lang.

Murphy, B. 1996. Computer corpora and vocabulary study. *Language Learning Journal* 14, 53–57.

Nesi, H., and Basturkmen, H. 2006. Lexical bundles and discourse signaling in academic lectures. *International Journal of Corpus Linguistics* 11, 283–304.

Nesselhauf, N. 2003. The use of collocations by advanced learners of English and some implications for teaching. *Applied Linguistics* 24, 223–42.

O'Keeffe, A., and Farr, F. 2003. Using language corpora in initial teacher education: Pedagogic issues and practical applications. *TESOL Quarterly* 37, 389–418.

O'Keeffe, A., McCarthy, M., and Carter, R. 2007. *From corpus to classroom: Language use and language teaching.* Cambridge: Cambridge University Press.

Partington, A. 1998. *Patterns and meanings: Using corpora for English language research and teaching.* Amsterdam: John Benjamins.

———. 2001. Corpus-based description in teaching and learning. In G. Aston, ed., *Learning with corpora*, pp. 63–84. Houston, Texas: Athelstan.

Qiao, H. L., and Sussex, R. 1996. Using the Longman mini-concordancer on tagged and parsed corpora, with special reference to their use as an aid to grammar learning. *System* 24 (1), 41–64.

Quaglio, P. 2009. *Television dialogue: The sitcom* Friends *versus natural conversation.* Amsterdam: John Benjamins.

Quaglio, P., and Biber, D. 2006. The grammar of conversation. In B. Aarts and A. McMahon, eds., *The handbook of English linguistics*, pp. 692–723. Oxford: Blackwell.

Quirk, R., Greenbaum, S., Leech, G., and Svartvik, J. 1972. *A grammar of contemporary English.* London: Longman.

Reder, S., Harris, K., and Setzler, K. 2003. A multimedia adult learner corpus. *TESOL Quarterly* 37, 546–57.

Renouf, A. 1997. Teaching corpus linguistics to teachers of English. In A. Wichmann, S. Fligelstone, T. McEnery, and G. Knowles, eds., *Teaching and language corpora*, pp. 255–66. London: Longman.

Reppen, R. 2001. Writing development among elementary students: Corpus based perspectives. In R. Simpson and J. Swales eds., *Corpus linguistics in North America*, pp. 211–25. Ann Arbor: University of Michigan Press.

Reppen, R., Fitzmaurice, S., and Biber D., eds. 2002. *Using corpora to explore linguistic variation.* Amsterdam: John Benjamins.

Reppen, R., and Simpson, R. 2002. Corpus linguistics. In N. Schmitt, ed., *An introduction to applied linguistics*, pp. 92–111. London: Arnold.

Reppen, R., and Vásquez, C. 2007. Using corpus linguistics to investigate the language of teacher training. In J. Walinski, K. Kredens, and S. Gozdz Roszkowski, eds., *Corpora and ICT in language studies*, pp. 13–29. Frankfurt: Peter Lang.

Ringbom, H. 1998. Vocabulary frequencies in advanced learner English: A cross-linguistic approach. In S. Granger, ed., *Learner English on computer*, pp. 41–52. London: Longman.

Robinson, M., Stoller, F., Constanza-Robinson, M., and Jones, J. 2008. *Write like a chemist*. New York: Oxford University Press.

Römer, U. 2005. *Progressives, patterns, pedagogy*. Amsterdam: John Benjamins.

Salsbury, T., and Crummer, C. 2008. Using teacher-developed corpora in the CBI classroom. *English Teaching Forum* 2, 28–37.

Sand, A. 1998. First findings from ICE-Jamaica: the verb phrase. In A. Renouf ed., *Explorations in corpus linguistics*, pp. 201–216. Amsterdam: Rodopi.

Schmidt, R. 1990. The role of consciousness in second language learning. *Applied Linguistics* 11, 129–58.

Schmitt, D., and Schmitt, N. 2005. *Focus on vocabulary*. Harlow, England: Longman.

Scovel, T. 2000. What I learned from the new Longman grammar. *CATESOL News* 323, 12–16.

Seidlhofer, S. 2000. Operationalizing intertextuality: Using learner corpora for learning. In L. Burnard and T. McEnery, eds., *Rethinking language pedagogy from a corpus perspective*, pp. 207–223. Frankfurt: Peter Lang.

Shirato, J., and Stapleton, P. 2007. Comparing English vocabulary in a spoken learner corpus with a native speaker corpus: Pedagogical implications arising from an empirical study in Japan. *Language Teaching Research* 11 (4), 393–412.

Simpson, R. 2004. Stylistic features of spoken academic discourse: The role of formulaic expressions. In U. Connor and T. Upton, eds., *Applied corpus linguistics: A multidimensional perspective*, pp. 37–64. Amsterdam: Rodopi.

Simpson, R., Lucka, B., and Ovens, J. 2000. Methodological challenges of planning a spoken corpus with pedagogical outcomes. In L. Burnard and T. McEnery, eds., *Rethinking language pedagogy from a corpus perspective*, pp. 43–49. Frankfurt: Peter Lang.

Simpson, R., and Mendis, D. 2003. A corpus-based study of idioms in academic speech. *TESOL Quarterly* 37, 419–41.

Simpson, R., and Swales, J. 2001. eds. *Corpus linguistics in North America: Selections from the 1999 symposium*. Ann Arbor: University of Michigan Press.

Sinclair, J. ed. 1987. *Looking up*. London: Collins.

———. 1991. *Corpus, concordance, collocation*. Oxford: Oxford University Press.

———. ed. 2004. *How to use corpora in language teaching*. Amsterdam: John Benjamins.

Stevens, V. 1993. Concordances as enhancements to language competence. *TESOL Matters* 2 (6), 11–21.

Stubbs, M. 1993. British traditions in text analysis: From Firth to Sinclair. In M. Baker, G. Francis, and E. Tognini-Bonelli, eds., *Text and technology*, pp. 1–33. Philadelphia: John Benjamins.

———. *Text and corpus analysis*. Oxford: Blackwell.

Swales, J. M. 2002. Integrated and fragmented worlds: EAP materials and corpus linguistics. In J. Flowerdew, ed., *Academic Discourse*, pp. 150–64. London: Longman, Pearson Education.

Swales, J., and Malczewski, B. 2001. Discourse management and new episode flags in MICASE. In Simpson, R., and Swales, J. eds., *Corpus linguistics in North America*, pp. 179–94. Ann Arbor: University of Michigan Press.

Thompson, P., and Tribble, C. 2001. Looking at citations: Using corpora in English for academic purposes. *Language Learning and Technology* 5 (3), 91–105.

Todd, R. 2001. Induction from self-selected concordances and self-correction. *System* 29 (1), 91–102.

Tono, Y. 2000. A computer learner corpus-based analysis of the acquisition order of English grammatical morphemes. In L. Burnard and T. McEnery, eds., *Rethinking language pedagogy from a corpus perspective*, pp. 123–32. Frankfurt: Peter Lang.

Tribble, C. 2001. Small corpora and teaching writing: Towards a corpus informed pedagogy of writing. In M. Ghadessy, H. Mohsen, A. Henry, and R. Roseberry, eds., *Small corpus studies and ELT: Theory and practice*, pp. 381–408. Amsterdam: John Benjamins.

Tribble, C., and Jones, G. 1997. *Concordances in the classroom*. Houston: Athelstan.

Virtanen, T. 1998. Direct questions in argumentative student writing. In S. Granger, ed., *Learner English on computer*, pp. 94–118. London: Longman.

Waring, R., and Nation, I. S. P. 1997. Vocabulary size, text coverage and word lists. In N. Schmitt and M. McCarthy, eds., *Vocabulary: Description, acquisition and pedagogy*, pp. 6–19. Cambridge: Cambridge University Press.

Weber, J. 2001. A concordance- and genre-informed approach to ESL essay writing. *ELT Journal* 55, 14–20.

West, M. 1953. *A general service list of English words*. London: Longman.

Wichmann, A. 1995. Using concordances for the teaching of modern languages in higher education. *Language Learning Journal* 11, 61–63.

Wichmann, A., Fligelstone, S., McEnery, T., and Knowles, G. eds. 1997. *Teaching and language corpora*. London: Longman.

Widdowson, H. 1996. Comment: Authenticity and autonomy in ELT. *ELT Journal* 50, 67–68.

Willis, J. 1998. Concordances in the classroom without a computer: Assembling and exploiting concordances of common words. In B. Tomlinson, ed., *Materials development in language teaching*, pp. 44–66. Cambridge: Cambridge University Press.

Wray, A. 2002. *Formulaic language and the lexicon*. Cambridge: Cambridge University Press.

Yoon, H., and Hirvela, A. 2004. ESL student attitudes toward corpus use in L2 writing. *Journal of Second-Language Writing* 13, 257–83.

Zanettin, F. 2001. Swimming in words: Corpora, translation, and language learning. In G. Aston ed., *Learning with corpora*, pp. 177–97. Houston, TX: Athelstan.

Zorzi, D. 2001. The pedagogic use of spoken corpora: Learning discourse markers in Italian. In G. Aston, ed., *Learning with corpora*, pp. 85–107. Houston, TX: Athelstan.

Some relevant journals

Applied Linguistics, Computational Linguistics, Computers in English Linguistics, Corpora, ELT, ESP, ICAME, International Journal of Corpus Linguistics, Journal of English Linguistics, Literary and Linguistic Computing, Language Learning and Technology (online journal), *System*

References

Aston, G., Bernardini, S., and Stewart, D. 2005. *Corpora and language learners*. Amsterdam: John Benjamins.

Baker, P., Hardie, A., and McEnery, T. 2006. *A glossary of corpus linguistics*. Edinburgh: Edinburgh Press.

Barlow, M. 2002. *MonoConc*. Houston, TX: Athelstan.

Biber, D. 1988. *Variation across speech and writing*. Cambridge: Cambridge University Press.

———. 1993. Representativeness in corpus design. *Literary and linguistic computing* 8: 243–57.

———. 2006. *University language: A corpus-based study of spoken and written registers*. Amsterdam: John Benjamins.

Biber, D., Conrad, S., and Cortes, V. 2004. If you look at . . . : Lexical bundles in university teaching and textbooks. *Applied Linguistics*, 25, 3: 371–405.

Biber, D., Conrad, S., and Reppen, R. 1998. *Corpus linguistics: Exploring language structure and use*. Cambridge: Cambridge University Press.

Biber, D., Conrad, S., Reppen, R., Byrd, P., Helt, M., Clark, V., Cortes, V., Csomay, E., and Urzua, A. 2004. *Representing language use in the university: Analysis of the TOEFL 2000 Spoken and Written Academic Language Corpus*. ETS TOEFL Monograph Series, MS-25. Princeton, NJ: Educational Testing Service.

Biber, D., Johansson, S., Leech, G., Conrad, S., and Finegan, E. 1999. *Longman grammar of spoken and written English*. London: Longman.

Biber, D., and Reppen, R. 2002. What does frequency have to do with grammar teaching? In *Studies in second language acquisition* 24, 199–208.

Byrd, P. 1995. *Material writer's guide*. Boston: Heinle and Heinle.

Cheng, W., Greaves, C., and Warren, M. 2008. *A corpus-driven study of discourse intonation: The Hong Kong corpus of spoken English*. Amsterdam: John Benjamins.

Conrad, S., and Biber, D. eds. 2001. *Variation in English: Multi-dimensional studies*. London: Longman.

Coxhead, A. 2000. A new academic word list. *TESOL Quarterly*, 34, 213–38.

Davis, M. 2007–. *Time* Magazine Corpus (100 million words, 1920s–2000s). Available online at http://corpus.byu.edu/time (accessed Aug. 21, 2009).

———. 2008–. COCA: Corpus of Contemporary American English (400 million words, 1990–2009). Available online at http://americancorpus.org (accessed Aug. 21, 2009).

Donley, K., and Reppen, R. 2001. Using corpus tools to highlight academic vocabulary in sustained content language teaching. *TESOL Journal*, Vol. 10, 2/3, 7–12.

Gavioli, L. 2001. The learner as researcher: Introducing corpus concordancing in the classroom. In G. Aston, ed., *Learning with corpora*, pp. 108–37. Houston, TX: Athelstan.

Gavioli, L., and Aston, G. 2001. Enriching reality: Language corpora in language pedagogy. *ELT Journal*, 55, 238–46.

Grabe, W. 2009. *Reading in a second language: Moving from theory to practice.* Cambridge: Cambridge University Press.

Grabe, W., and Stoller, F. 2001. *Teaching and researching reading.* Harlow: Pearson Longman.

Huntley, H. 2006. *Essential academic vocabulary.* Boston: Houghton Mifflin Co.

Johns, T. 1994. From printout to handout: Grammar and vocabulary teaching in the context of data-driven learning. In T. Odlin, ed., *Perspectives on pedagogical grammar*, pp. 293–313. Cambridge: Cambridge University Press.

Kennedy, G. 1998. *An introduction to corpus linguistics.* London: Longman.

McCarthy, M., McCarten, J., and Sandiford, H. 2004/2006. *Touchstone* Level 1, Level 2, Level 3, Level 4. Cambridge: Cambridge University Press.

McCarthy, M., and O'Dell, F. 2010. *Basic vocabulary in use.* Cambridge: Cambridge University Press.

McDonough, J., and Shaw, C. 1993. *Materials and methods in ELT: A teacher's guide.* Oxford, England: Blackwell.

McEnery, T., and Wilson, A. 1996. *Corpus linguistics.* Edinburgh: Edinburgh University Press.

Meyer, C. 2002. *English corpus linguistics.* Cambridge: Cambridge University Press.

Mindt, D. 1998. Corpora and the teaching of English in Germany. In G. Knowles, T. McEnery, S. Fligelstone, and A. Wichman, eds., *Teaching and language corpora*, pp. 40–50. London: Longman.

Moon, R. 1998. *Fixed expressions and idioms in English: A corpus-based approach.* Oxford: Oxford University Press.

Nation, I. S. P. 2007. Vocabulary learning through experience tasks. *Language Forum* 33, 2: 33–43.

O'Keefe, A., McCarthy, M., and Carter, R. 2007. *From corpus to classroom.* Cambridge: Cambridge University Press.

Reppen, R., and Simpson, R. 2002. Corpus linguistics. In N. Schmitt, ed., *An introduction to applied linguistics*, 92–111. London: Arnold.

Schmitt, N. 2000. Key concepts in ELT: Lexical chunks. *English Language Teaching Journal* 54, 4: 400–401.

———. ed. 2004. *Formulaic sequences.* Amsterdam: John Benjamins.

———. 2008. Instructed second language vocabulary learning. *Language Teaching Research* 12, 3: 329–63.

Schmitt, N., and McCarthy, M. eds. 1997. *Vocabulary: Description, acquisition, and pedagogy.* Cambridge: Cambridge University Press.

Schmitt, D., and Schmitt, N. 2005. *Focus on vocabulary.* New York: Longman.

Simpson, R. C., Briggs, S. L., Ovens, J., and Swales, J. M. 2002. The Michigan Corpus of Academic Spoken English. Ann Arbor, MI: The Regents of the University of Michigan. micase.elicorpora.info (accessed Aug. 21, 2009).

Simpson, R., and Swales, J. eds. 2001. *Corpus linguistics in North America: Selections from the 1999 symposium.* Ann Arbor: University of Michigan Press.

Sinclair, J. ed. 2004. *How to use corpora in language teaching.* Amsterdam: John Benjamins.

Index

academic vocabulary *see* vocabulary
  development
Academic Word List
  dictionaries, use in, 17
  vocabulary books, 19–20, 29
  vocabulary instruction, 14, 36–7, 68
academic writing *see* writing
affixes activity, 23–5
alphabetical order word lists, 5, 7–8, 7t
American National Corpus (ANC), 5, 83

Biber, D., 4, 11, 22, 23, 25, 28, 44, 65t,
  70, 71
British National Corpus (BNC), 3, 4, 83
Brown corpus, 3
Business Letter Concordancer (BLC), 85

chunks *see* lexical bundles
co-occurrence patterns, 11, 25
Cobb, T., 36
COCA *see* Corpus of Contemporary
  American English
Collins Cobuild Corpus Concordance
  Sampler, 85
Collocate, 85
collocations, 11, 25
Compleat Lexical Tutor, 5, 36–7, 85
concordance lines, using
  co-occurrence patterns, 11
  lines generated, display of, 8–10
  patterns of use, insights into, 8, 11
  sample activity, 10–11
  tagged texts, use of, 11–12
  see also KWICs (Key Word in Context
    indexes)
Concordancing, 85–6
Conc, 85
Conrad, S., 11, 44
conversation

foundational, 70–1
  lexical bundles, and use of fillers, 65–6
  nonacademic situations, 70
Cool Edit, 58, 87
corpora creation, for classroom use
  corpus size, 55
  goal, need for clear, 54
  representativeness, 55
  spoken texts, transcription of, 58–9
  text collection, 55–60
  written texts, original and 'clean'
    versions of, 57–8
Corpus Lab Web site, 37
Corpus of Contemporary American
  English (COCA), 3, 4, 37, 38
  conversation activity, 65
  display format, 39–40
  grammatical searches, 39–41
  KWICs of target form, 41
  language exploration activities, 77–8
  register awareness activities, 46–9, 63
  register comparison searches, 39–40
  Web site, 83
  written *versus* spoken language
    activity, 66–7
Corpus of Spoken American English
  (CSPAE), 83
corpus, definition of, 2–4
Corpus.BYU.edu, 83
Coxhead, A., 20

Davies, M., 39
dictionaries, corpus-informed, 16–17,
  19–20, 36
Donley, K.M., 68

English for International Students Unit
  (ESIU), University of Birmingham,
  33–4

CPSIA information can be obtained
at www.ICGtesting.com
Printed in the USA
LVOW04s1746150116

469972LV00008B/52/P